Helen Hopkins Crandell Award

for

Sustained Excellence in Creative Writing

to

Rhoda Mildred Buchler

Washington Irving High School

June, 1949

FLOWERS OF EVIL

✻

FLOWERS OF EVIL

FROM THE FRENCH OF

CHARLES BAUDELAIRE

By

GEORGE DILLON

*

EDNA ST. VINCENT MILLAY

With the Original Texts
and with a Preface by

Miss Millay

HARPER & BROTHERS PUBLISHERS

NEW YORK   LONDON

FLOWERS OF EVIL

PREFACE

MANY WRITERS, I am sure, will envy me the happy circumstance which makes it possible for me so highly to praise and so warmly to recommend this book of which I am co-author, without at the same time laying myself open to the grave charge of liking my own book and saying so. The circumstance which permits—permits, do I say?—which imposes upon me this heady and exhilarating task is the following:

Until four months ago this was entirely George Dillon's book; I had no part in it. For nearly two years Mr. Dillon had had the intention of bringing out a book of his translations of the poems of Charles Baudelaire. He had sent me several of the translations which were already finished, and asked me if I liked them sufficiently to be willing to write an introduction for them. I had seen some excellent translations of French poetry into English,[1] but I had never seen a translation of *Les Fleurs du Mal* which greatly pleased me.[2] I found Mr. Dillon's poems so impressive in themselves, considered as English poetry, so true to the original in style, as well as in matter and mood, that I replied saying I should be delighted and honoured to write the introduction. Mr. Dillon continued with his translating; and I went on with my own work. I was familiar with the writings of the great French poet, and admired him extremely; but I had never translated a line of Baude-

[1] Swinburne and Andrew Lang, among others, did beautiful work in this line; George Santayana's inspired rendering of Gautier's *l'Art* is a model for translators.

[2] The Arthur Symons version, for instance, which is probably the best known, is shockingly inaccurate and misleading.

[v]

laire, nor had I ever considered doing so, although I had made a few translations from certain other French writers.

About four months ago, when looking up a poem in *Les Fleurs du Mal*, in order to compare the original with Mr. Dillon's English version of it, my attention was caught by a line in quite another poem; and a few minutes later, with something of the terror which a person must feel who realizes that he has undoubtedly been bitten by a mosquito and that he is in a notoriously malarial climate, I found *that I had translated the line!*

That in itself would have been innocent enough, but I was aware that I was breathing hard, that I more likely than not had a feverish glitter in my eye, that I had entirely forgotten what I was looking up, and that I had more than half an idea as to how the translation of the whole stanza should go!

"Now, that's perfectly all right, and don't you be worried," I said to myself soothingly and with a false smile; "you're just doing it for fun; it's just an exercise. Go right ahead and translate the whole poem. It won't do you a bit of harm. Only, of course, when you've done that, you'll go straight back to work on your own book, which is *the most important thing in the world to you*, and you won't even *think* of translating another."

This is what I said to myself, but neither of us believed me. Fatally in my mind was the sickening conviction that I was in for it, that I had caught the fever, and that neither quinine nor wise counsel could save me.

From that day to this moment I have thought of nothing, lived for nothing, but my translations from *Les Fleurs du Mal* which are now printed, together with George Dillon's, in this collection (the combined translations representing about one-half of Baudelaire's published poetry).

I see no reason, however, why the writer of a preface to another

person's book should be restrained, just because against his will and
propelled by a demon he has burst into the book proper and become a part of it, from writing his preface.

Which I now proceed to do.

I

To translate poetry into prose, no matter how faithfully and
even subtly the words are reproduced, is to betray the poem. To
translate formal stanzas into free verse, free verse into rhymed
couplets, is to fail the foreign poet in a very important way.

With most poets, the shape of the poem is not an extraneous at-
tribute of it: the poem could not conceivably have been written in
any other form. When the image of the poem first rises before the
suddenly quieted and intensely agitated person who is to write it, its
shadowy bulk is already dimly outlined; it is rhymed or unrhymed;
it is trimeter, tetrameter, or pentameter; it is free verse, a sonnet,
an epic, an ode, a five-act play. To many poets, the physical character of their poem, its rhythm, its rhyme, its music, the way it
looks on the page, is quite as important as the thing they wish to
say; to some it is vastly more important. To translate the poetry of
E. E. Cummings into the rhymed alexandrines of Molière, would
be to do Mr. Cummings no service.

Yet this is precisely the sort of thing which is done in a majority
of instances when poetry is translated from one language into another. The translator takes the poem, no matter what its form may
be, and forces it into the meter and form to which he is most accustomed, the one in which he writes most easily. There are notable
exceptions (John Payne and W. J. Robertson, for example, both
of whom have translated into alexandrines and managed them very
skilfully). But for the most part the translator—and no wonder—
gives himself every possible help and advantage at the outset; a

[vii]

French poet translating verse, no matter what its metrical scheme may be, into French, will, ninety-nine times out of a hundred, translate it into alexandrines; an English poet will translate alexandrines into pentameter. In *Les Fleurs du Mal* there are only two poems in lines of ten syllables—*Le Léthé*, which opens this collection, and *Le Portrait*, which appears further on.

Baudelaire made, so far as I know, only one translation of English poetry into French, with the exception of Poe's *The Raven*, which he translated into prose. This, unexpectedly enough, was an "imitation" of part of Longfellow's *Hiawatha*.[1] It is difficult to imagine what it was in the American poem which attracted a poet who not only in his own quality was at the opposite pole from Longfellow, but whose two great enthusiasms in English were the works of Edgar Allan Poe and Thomas De Quincey's *Confessions of an English Opium Eater*. Since it is only that part of the poem called *The Peace Pipe* which he seems to have been concerned with, it is possible that it was the theme of universal brotherhood which attracted him; it is also possible that it was principally the strange meter and rhythm of the lines. In any case, Baudelaire's imitation of *Hiawatha* is in the traditional meter of the Comédie-Française— it is in alexandrines, and it is rhymed.

Consider these lines from the original:

On the Mountains of the Prairie,
On the great Red Pipe-Stone Quarry,

[1] I think it is not generally known by Americans that the American poet Edgar Allan Poe, who is so well known in Europe through Baudelaire's translations of his work into French, and so greatly admired there, is known there for the most part, except by those who have read his poetry in English, as a writer of tales. Baudelaire, who admired Poe so enormously, and who made it the work of nearly half his writing life to present Poe to the French reading public, presented him only as a writer of prose; he did not translate Poe's poetry.

Gitche Manito, the mighty,
He the Master of Life, descending,
On the red crags of the quarry
Stood erect, and called the nations,
Called the tribes of men together.

.   .   .   .   .   .

From the red stone of the quarry
With his hand he broke a fragment,
Moulded it into a pipe-head,
Shaped and fashioned it with figures;
From the margin of the river
Took a long reed for a pipe-stem,
With its dark green leaves upon it;
Filled the pipe with bark of willow,
With the bark of the red willow.

This is Baudelaire's approximation of them:

Or Gitche Manito, le Maître de la Vie,
Le Puissant, descendit dans la verte prairie,
Dans l'immense prairie aux coteaux montueux;
Et là, sur les rochers de la Rouge Carrière,
Dominant tout l'espace et baigné de lumière,
Il se tenait debout, vaste et majestueux.

Alors it convoqua les peuples innombrables,
Plus nombreux que ne sont les herbes et les sables.
Avec sa main terrible il rompit un morceau
Du rocher, dont il fit une pipe superbe,
Puis, au bord du ruisseau, dans une enorme gerbe,
Pour s'en faire un tuyau, choisit un long roseau.

[ix]

Having read Baudelaire's *Calumet de Paix*, what does the French reader know about an American poem called *Hiawatha?* He knows that once there were some redskins, and they were very war-like, and they had a god whose name was Gitche Manito, and he was distressed because they were so warlike, so he made a Pipe of Peace, and they all smoked it. He feels also, such will have been the spell of Baudelaire's lovely lines upon him, that all this was very important. But of the poem *Hiawatha* itself, of what made it a poem, he knows nothing. All the charm of Longfellow's drum-beating, double-stamping, moccasin-shod tetrameter is lost in the courtly alexandrine of the French adaptation.

When George Dillon wrote me that he was translating some of *Les Fleurs du Mal* into English verse, and that he was using in every instance the meter and the form used by Baudelaire in the original poem, I was very much interested; this had always seemed to me the only way to go about such a task. It is true that the trans-lator, who is hard put to it enough in any case to transpose a poem from one language into another without strangling it in the process, here takes upon himself an added burden; but he is more than re-warded when he finds that his translation, when read aloud directly after the original, echoes the original, that it is still, in some miraculous way, the same poem, although its words are now in a different language. One impertinence at least, of the many im-pertinences almost necessarily involved in re-writing another per-son's poem, has not been committed: the poem has been pretty roughly handled, possibly, but its anatomy at least is still intact.

I do not mean by this to suggest that the more closely the trans-lator adheres to the rhythm and the rhyme-scheme of the original, the more liberties he may permit himself in the over-setting of the mood and physical content, of the actual words, of the original. No. It is to be supposed that the translator is a serious person, probably

[x]

greatly admiring, and in any case deeply respecting, the poem upon which he is engaged. It is his duty, as it is his delight, to reproduce this poem in its every aspect as faithfully as possible. To realize, as he works, that his poem is beginning to look like the original, and in a way even to suggest the sound of it, gives him added courage to proceed with his strenuous and exacting task.

Poetry should not, and indeed cannot properly be translated except by poets. But there is more to it than that; it is as complicated as blood-transfusion. It is doubtful if any English poet could translate equally well the poems of Pierre de Ronsard, Victor Hugo, Alfred de Musset and Charles Baudelaire. It is quite conceivable that William Wordsworth could have made an excellent translation of the poems of Victor Hugo; but one drop of the blood of Wordsworth in the veins of Baudelaire would have meant death. Baudelaire himself was so eminently fitted to translate the works of Poe that one feels sometimes when reading the translation that Edgar Poe wrote his own stories both in English and French, and one is not sure in which language one prefers them. But Baudelaire in his imitation of Longfellow was not so successful. Quite apart from the question of meter, a natural, unbridgeable gulf existed between the minds and the tastes of the French and American poets.

You will note that where Longfellow says simply, "Gitche Manito, the mighty . . . Stood erect . . ." Baudelaire says, "Dominating all space and bathed in light, he stood erect, vast and majestic." Naturally, the work of making an eight-syllable line into a twelve-syllable line, supposing that the equivalent words in the two languages are of about the same length, as in this instance for the most part they happen to be, includes a considerable elaboration. But it would have been more characteristic of Longfellow to enlarge, not upon the god-like qualities of Gitche Manito, but upon the physical attributes of natural objects. Compare the two descriptions of the making of the Peace Pipe. Longfellow says, "From the red stone of the quarry With his hand he broke a fragment"; Baudelaire says, "With his *terrible* hand he broke a piece of the *rock*"; the italics are mine, I put them there to call attention to the fact that in the French poem "the red stone of the quarry" becomes plain "rock," whereas the simple "hand" of Gitche Manito becomes a "terrible" hand. Take the following two lines from *Hiawatha:* "Moulded it into a pipe-head, Shaped and fashioned it with figures." What does Baudelaire say? "He made a superb pipe." Continue with this for a moment: "Took a long reed for a pipe-stem, With its dark green leaves upon it"; "To make himself a stem from it, he chose a long reed"; "Filled the pipe with bark of willow, With the bark of the red willow"; "To fill it he took the willow's bark"—this last is from the third stanza of *Le Calumet de Paix*, not quoted here. (These brutal prose renderings of Baudelaire's lines, naturally, give no suggestion of the quality of *Le Calumet de Paix* as a poem. But I am considering it here not as a poem, but just as a translation.)

As I shall point out further on in this preface, for Baudelaire to consider the reed and the willow at all was a great concession to Longfellow; that he should concern himself as to whether or not so dull a creature as a reed had "dark green leaves" or as to what *kind* of willow it was, that was asking a bit too much of him.

Under the pen of Baudelaire not only do the "groves of Tuscaloosa" become a "perfumed" forest, and the simple "morning" through whose "tranquil air" the smoke of the peace pipe mounts a "vermilion" morning; but in the last line of *Le Calumet de Paix* Gitche Manito himself, of whom Longfellow says he "Vanished from before their faces In the smoke that rolled around him, The Pukwana of the Peace Pipe," ascends into heaven not only "immense," "sublime," "radiant," but also "perfumed"! There was here an insuperable incompatibility of temperaments.

The poet best fitted, technically, to translate the work of a foreign poet, is the accomplished and disciplined craftsman in his own tongue, who possesses also a comprehensive knowledge of the language from which he is translating. All his skill, however, will not avail him, if he is not sufficiently in sympathy with the poem he is translating, to feel that he might have written it himself. The poem may be even strikingly different from his own work; yet he must feel, at least during the period at which he is at work upon it, that he might have written it himself. He must be able to fill the veins of the poem, nearly emptied through the wound inflicted by translation, with his own blood, and make the poem breathe again.

To be attracted by the music of a poem, to admire it as a fine piece of observation, to concede that the thought expressed is subtle, and that the meter and rhyme are extremely well managed —all these honest approbations will not avail, will not lift a finger to save, in his difficult task, the translator nagged by the consideration that the work upon which he is engaged is not "strictly moral," must at all costs be kept from the clairvoyant eyes of the young, and that *really*, dash it all, the fellow couldn't *possibly* have meant some of the things he said!

It would seem that certain translators of the *Fleurs du Mal* have been at times rather uncomfortable under their self-shouldered pack. One sees them at moments ill at ease and embarrassed in the face of a scandalous or otherwise disturbing line, and at these moments the unforgivable thing is bound to happen: they gloss him over; they tone him down; they pass him off. They translate him with the lights out.

Charles Baudelaire did not live the kind of life which would have

[xiii]

recommended him to doting fathers as a fitting companion for their débutante daughters— (although in truth, those débutante daughters would have been even comically safe with him: he was not interested in the undeveloped and immature). He lived openly from the time he was twenty-two with a woman of the lowest class, to whom he was not married; he published a book of poems which was instantly seized by the police as being a menace to public morals; and he took opium. An awareness of this author's reprehensible habits seems at times to have stood between the translator and the particular poem under consideration, as it often, unfortunately, stands between the poem and the reader. Let a poem of Baudelaire be filled with the most rarefied and ethereal sentiments toward some woman, with the deepest and most tender sympathy for the afflicted and the poor, with the most fervent and ecstatic religious ecstasy—no, no; walk all around it carefully! prod it with a stick at arm's length and be ready to jump! if you pick it up at all, pick it up by the tail.

Even to this day, and even in France, where he is so widely read and so greatly admired, Baudelaire is considered a monster. A very cultured Frenchwoman said to me a few days ago, "But Baudelaire was *never* tender! *C'était un monstre!*"

One wonders sometimes what the critic of literature would do, were he left entirely in the dark as to the sex, age, amorous proclivities and political affiliations of the writer whose work he is considering. Fortunately, he does not often find himself in this predicament. For the most part he is in the enviable position of the graphologist who writes, "Send me a sample of your handwriting, and I will read your character," having just looked one up in *Who's Who*, skimmed through one's recently published autobiography, and had an hour or so's ever-so-interesting conversation with one's most garrulous friend.

[xiv]

It is impossible to make a good translation of a poet of whom one disapproves. To excuse him or to condemn him is, for the translator, equally impertinent and equally fatal. The poem is the thing. Is it interesting?—is it beautiful?—is it sublime? Then it was written by nobody. It exists by itself. The reader of poetry who has never had the brain-dizzying experience of being seduced into stupefied, into incredulous, into dismayed, into amused, into delighted, into wild unqualified enthusiasm for a poem written by his bitterest personal enemy, or by the person whom he has for years considered to be the Most Sickening Poet on the Face of the Earth, has never known one of the few authentic paradisiacal vertigos of life.

I did not know whether George Dillon approved, deplored or was indifferent to the much-discussed bad habits of Charles Baudelaire, or what his opinion might be as to the effect upon the public morals of *Les Fleurs du Mal*. But in the course of several years of friendship Mr. Dillon and I had read and discussed much poetry together. Our arguments had been fiery and abusive; frigid and polite; pitying and tolerant; scornful and amused; but never had the consideration of the poet's domestic arrangements, or of his poetry as possibly conducive to or deterrent from evil practices, entered into our discussions of his poems as such.

Baudelaire wrote in his projected preface to the second edition of *Les Fleurs du Mal*, "Some people have said to me that these poems might do harm; I am not rejoiced by this. Others, worthy souls, that they might do good; and that did not afflict me. The fears of the former and the hopes of the latter equally astonished me." I felt sure that the fact that several of the *Fleurs du Mal* would be rather out of place on the bookshelf in the nursery, would not strongly influence this translator in his consideration of Baudelaire's poetry, or lead him, to use the author's own phrase, "to con-

[xv]

fuse ink with virtue." Moreover I felt that in this instance, between the French and American poets there was a real, though not necessarily complete, temperamental compatibility, which would make it possible for Mr. Dillon not only to understand and sympathize with the mood and point of view of many of the poems in the *Fleurs du Mal*, but even perhaps in some cases to re-create them.

I was not disappointed. When I read *Le Mort Joyeux*, *Le Léthé*, *Le Gout du Néant*, *Lesbos*, *L'Examen de Minuit*, *De Profundis Clamavi*, as they appear in translation in this book, it seemed to me that the tortured and idealistic spirit of Charles Baudelaire himself was in these English lines.

II

To say that all French poetry is written in hexameter and all English poetry in pentameter, is to exaggerate, but is not to give a false impression.[1] It is true that Villon, in the fifteenth century, did not write in hexameter, almost all his poetry being in lines of eight syllables, with here and there a poem in ten-syllable lines. But Pierre de Ronsard, writing just a century later, in addition to writing many poems in ten-syllable lines, etc., wrote copiously in alexandrines; and in his half-letter, half-essay, the *Abbrégé de l'Art Poétique François*, he wrote to the Abbé Alphonse Delbène, "Alexandrines hold that place in our language which heroic verse held among the Greeks and Latins; they are composed of twelve or thirteen syllables: the masculine of twelve, the feminine of thirteen; and always have their rest on the sixth syllable. . . ." Further on

[1] The French alexandrine is not, properly speaking, hexameter at all, although a line of twelve syllables. Yet the nearest thing to it that we have in English is the iambic hexameter; and if I refer to the alexandrine at times as a line of hexameter, I do this in order to make myself more immediately intelligible to the English reader.

he states that it is he who is responsible for definitely establishing the alexandrine in France: "Alexandrines, which, as you know, I brought into vogue and honour."

Hexameter is the traditional poetic form of the French, as pentameter of the English. All the dramas of Racine and Corneille were written in alexandrines, as were, except when they were written in prose, all the plays of Molière. All the plays of Shakespeare were written, with the exception of a few lines, in pentameter, as were his longer poems and all his sonnets.[1] Chaucer's *Canterbury Tales* were written in pentameter, as was his *Troilus and Cressida;* the *Paradise Lost* of Milton is in pentameter, as is almost everything that Milton wrote; Wordsworth's *The Prelude* and *The Excursion* are in pentameter; the great poems of Shelley and Keats are in five-foot lines.

The alexandrine in English poetry is for the most part perfectly at home and lives with all its gracious dignity and power, only under one condition: when employed as the ninth line of the famous stanza invented by Edmund Spenser, the first eight lines of which are in pentameter. Spenser used this beautiful stanza in the *Faerie Queen*, Shelley in *The Revolt of Islam*, Keats in the lovely *Eve of St. Agnes*. Outside this use of the line, the iambic hexameter has not often, so far as I know, been used in English poetry, and seldom with much success. (The *dactylic* hexameter of the Greek and Latin epics, which Longfellow imitated in his poem *Evangeline*, is quite a different thing.)

The poet setting out to translate French hexameter into English hexameter, is at once confronted by a problem which he would not encounter were he translating from the German, the Spanish, the Italian, the Russian, the Dutch. French words, of course, look like

[1] With the exception of one. One sonnet, in *The Passionate Pilgrim*, is in alexandrines.

this: *déréglé, bêtise, païen, forçat, espèce, héroïque*. But all these marks, all these jots and tittles, which make it so difficult for us to write in French on our American typewriters, are not used to emphasize one syllable of a word above another, but to show rather how the vowels are to be pronounced, whether they are long or short, etc.; the *accent circonflexe* over the *e* in *bêtise* indicates that in the course of the development of the language an *s* has been dropped between the *e* and the following *t*, and that the *e* must now carry all the stress which the *es* carried formerly—the word *bestial*, which has not lost the *s*, does not bear the accent; in old French *être* was *estre, fantôme* was *fantosme, blé* was *bled*.

In English, as in every other language with which I have the slightest acquaintance, with the exception of French, every word of more than one syllable has a definite and fixed stress on one of its syllables; if it is a long word it has also a secondary accent on some other one of its syllables; "morning" has its stress on the first syllable, "impede" on the second; this stress goes along with the word, like Mary's little lamb, into every phrase, into every line of poetry, it is a part of the word. A French word of no matter how many syllables has practically no accent at all on any of its syllables, and what faint accent it may have is easily lost in the accent of the phrase.

The *Grammaire de l'Académie française*, published in 1932, says: "The tonic accent consists in a greater intensity of one of the vowels of a word; one pronounces it more strongly than the other vowels. . . . This accent . . . is rather weak in French. . . . In polysyllables, the accent falls upon the last syllable pronounced: *vaisseau, tapage*. It must be observed that the intensity of the accent varies according to the importance of the word in a phrase and the place which it occupies there." The *French Grammar* of Fraser and Squair says: "In French, the syllables are uttered with

[xviii]

almost equal force, a very slight stress falling on the last syllable
of a word of two or more syllables. . . . Note.—In connected dis-
course the rule above stated varies considerably. . . . The safest
practise for the beginner is to pronounce all syllables with almost
equal force." (I am aware, of course, that many readers will know
a great deal more about all this than I do, and will think my little
exposition very childish and quaint; but I find that many people
who know French very well, have never given a thought to these
simple facts, without a consideration of which nothing I say from
now on would be understood.)

Consider now this opening line of a poem of Baudelaire which
I wished to translate into English hexametric verse:

"La servante au grand coeur dont vous étiez jalouse"

What am I to do with this?

I cannot translate it:

"The big-hearted servant of whom you were jealous" unless I
wish to follow it with some such line as

"Was not such a slut as the other maids tell us"!

Regardless of the fact that I have put into my line just the
proper number of syllables, twelve, to make up an alexandrine, and
have even been careful to put the caesura in the right place, nevertheless the line refuses to be an alexandrine; it is not hexameter, it
is tetrameter; the strong tonic accents of the English words have
determined the number of feet in the line. The natural way for an
English reader to read it is to give it four feet, of which three are
dactyls:

$$\bar{\ }\ \smile\ \smile\ \bar{\ }\ \smile\ \smile\ \bar{\ }\ \smile\ \smile\ \bar{\ }\ \smile$$
"The big-hearted servant of whom you were jealous"

A Frenchman would read the line as follows, accenting only the
second syllable of "servant" and the second syllable of "jealous":

"The-big-heart-ed-ser-*vant*//of-whom-you-were-jeal-*ous*"

Does the reader begin to perceive the translator's difficulty?

[xix]

I rendered the line as follows:

"The servant that we had, you were so jealous of."

This line, in spite of the irrepressible accent on the first syllables of "servant" and "jealous", approximates the French alexandrine.[1]

Being thus handicapped from the outset in our enterprise of making English verse sound like French verse, being obliged to force English words into a metrical scheme where they had not so far been signally happy, we soon found that we often came much closer to the effect we wanted by importing into the twelve-syllable line—wherever, due to certain unavoidably accented words, it seemed bumpy and unbalanced—one or two (infrequently three) extra syllables, still always keeping the line, however, a line of six feet.

The following line will give an example:

"Sometimes, to entertain themselves, the men of the crew"

Also we found, which Baudelaire himself had found, that to have the caesura fall invariably after the sixth syllable, as classically it must, could make a poem sound very stilted and dull; and we sometimes varied the position of the caesura.

Baudelaire, however, never quite abandoned the caesura after the sixth syllable, even when the main break in the line was elsewhere. Between the sixth and seventh syllables in his verses there is always a break, at least for the eye—what might be called an "honorary caesura"—that is, the sixth and seventh syllables are never syllables in the same word. Baudelaire never did this sort of thing:

"You are a lovely, rosy, lucid autumn sky"

1 In translating *La Prière d'un Païen*, I was unable to retain the Latin line: *Diva! supplicem exaudi!* Even had I avoided the elision, as Baudelaire, following the mediaeval Latin custom, has done, there would still be the tonic accents against me: *exaudi* would still rhyme with "rowdy". The French disregard the tonic accents, and stress the last syllable of *exaudi*.

Nor did he ever, indeed, write a line of hexameter with more than the classic twelve to thirteen syllables. Even had he wished to do so, he would not have been able to. French words possessing no accent, broadly speaking, in themselves, the two extra syllables of a fourteen-syllable line would not have fallen into dactyls, as they so readily do in English poetry—the fourteen syllable line would simply have become heptameter.

The person setting out to translate metrical verse into prose has an entirely different kind of work to do. Not being constrained at all by rhyme or meter, permitted to use, if he finds it necessary or even convenient, forty lines of prose as against twenty lines of poetry, it is definitely his business to give us what is known as a "literal" translation; since he is giving us nothing of the poem except what the poet *said*, he must tell us *exactly* what the poet said, leaving out nothing, adding nothing; this is practically the only value his work can have for us. The same thing holds true of the translating of metrical verse into free verse, except that here the translator has an added privilege—the privilege of making his translation a poem so sensuously beautiful in itself that, while it in no formal sense resembles the original at all, we are impressed by the fact that it is poetry, not prose, which he is translating, and that it is apparently very beautiful poetry; he has this added privilege, I say, of doing a special service to the original poem. He must not, however, because of this added privilege, be excited into the belief that he has an accompanying added freedom as far as faithfully rendering the text is concerned; since he is free to mould his translation into whatever shape may most please him, being no more bound by the form of the original than is the translator into prose, each being governed only by his own ear, his own taste, his own sense of balance and proportion, he, also, is required to present us with a faithful rendering of the text. This need not, indeed it often cannot be a rendering of word for word; but he must give us much more than the gist of the original poem; he must give us the strictest equivalent that he is able to produce, without omissions, without padding.

The statement that often a translation *cannot* be a rendering of word for word holds for all translations, the prose translation included. This impossibility rises from the fact that there are certain words existing in one language which do not exist in the other. The example of the English word "home" is familiar to everybody. The French have no word which means "home." They are so well aware of the lack of this word in their language that they are gradually taking over the English word. It is to be found in their standard dictionary, the Larousse, and is given as follows: *home, mot anglais signifiant* maison, *employé pour désigner le chez-soi, la famille, la vie intime*. It is even found in the abridged form of this dictionary. And more and more one sees the word—always looking rather forlorn and reproachful and extremely funny, like a dog in ruffles—above the doorways of hotels and boarding-houses in France: *Le Home; Le Home Sans Souci; Le Home Maréchal Foch.*

French people, a few generations from now, will very likely use the word "home" as naturally as they use any other word in their vocabulary, unaware that there was ever a time when their language was without it. But today they are still conscious when they use it that it is a foreign word. And the French translator detailed by his employer to translate "Home, Sweet Home" into French, will be pardoned if he does a little gesticulating.

There are, on the other hand, words in French, which the English language cannot approximate. How, for instance, am I to translate the Frenchman's expression *"mon pays"?* I cannot translate it as "my country"; when I say "my country", I mean "my country, 'tis of thee"; I mean the United States of America. But the Frenchman, when he says *"mon pays"*, is not thinking of France; France is *"la patrie."* He is thinking of a part of Normandie, a part of Provence, bounded by no lines visible on any map, bounded only by the horizon of his early associations, made significant for him by the simple and marvellous events of his childhood and adolescence; it is the part of the world he "comes from". To *"La France"* he gives his loyalty, his patriotism; if necessary, his life. But what he really loves is *"son pays."*

How can I render this into English? I cannot say "my state", "my county". I was born in the state of Maine; but the state of Maine is very big; I have not picked mayflowers on every hillside of its many rocky hillsides; I have not steamed clams in seaweed on every spruce-wooded island off its coast; no, it is not quite that. But sometimes, when motoring up along the shore of Maine, after we have passed Wiscasset, when we are coming to Waldoboro and Thomaston, when I know that only a few miles further on are Rockland, Rockport, Union, Camden, I say to my companion— in French, because there is no way of saying it in English—*"C'est mon pays."*

The person translating a French poem into English, if he comes across such a phrase as this, will perhaps be able to give something of its quality to his reader if he has an unlimited number of syllables in which to do so. If, however, he has made it an indispensable part of his translation to reproduce the meter and form of the French poem, it will be extremely difficult, usually impossible, for him to give an impression of what this phrase means without omitting entirely to consider some other phrase or phrases contained in the original. In such an emergency it will be physically impossible for him to give what is called a "literal" translation.

[xxiii]

He will be forced to decide for himself just what it was, stripped bare to its bone, which the poet wished to express; and he will then proceed to write his English poem, putting into it the bone complete, and as much of its lovely vestment as he can.

The worst translation, obviously, other things being equal, is the one which sounds the most as if it were a translation. It is the office of the translator to represent the original poem as faithfully as possible, not only in its mood, its matter, its structure, and its rhythm, but also in its freshness, its sincerity, its vigour, its ease. And the original poem is not a translation! Therefore the translation must not be a translation, either!—it must not appear to be.

It will perhaps by this time have occurred to the reader that the translator who embarks upon his enterprise with such a weighty cargo of principles and stern ideals may, if he runs into heavy weather, find himself in difficulties, and that in these circumstances one thing or another will very likely have to go by the board. The reader will be quite right about this. More times, many more times, than once, in the course of the preparation of this book, that is just what has happened. And the bitter question always was, of course, "What shall I jettison?"

In certain of the poems in this collection the translator, without being called upon to disturb at all the meter and the form of the original poem, has been able to produce a truly literal translation, a translation as close to the text as even a translator into prose could be required to give. This phenomenon, however, this blessed and ever earnestly invoked phenomenon, shows itself only at rare intervals, when the two languages, which have been at each other's throats for weeks, become suddenly mild and tractable, become like two old friends who have shared since childhood the difficult and perilous business of growing up, and who no longer have any secrets from each other—if there are four words that rhyme in the French text, why, there are four words that rhyme in the English, too, and which are their exact equivalent; it is as simple as that.

But some of the translations included in this book are so free as to be more properly speaking adaptations than translations. My rendering of *La Lune Offensée* is an extreme example of free translation. I could, I think, explain to the satisfaction of the reader why I felt it desirable to omit the phrase *"lampe de nos repaires"*, to sacrifice entirely the "yellow domino" and the "clandestine foot", in order to have space in which more fully to develop (a) the insolence of the poet to the moon, (b) the picture of the poet's mother. But there are other things which I wish to talk about; and I must not make this preface too long, for I want it to be read.

I will say only, in conclusion of this part of my subject, that the reader of these poems who does not know much French, and who wishes to brush up on his French by comparing the original with the translation, will possibly find himself after the study of a few phrases puzzled if not definitely embarrassed. For where the author says (he does not actually say this; this is just by way of illustration), "Sapphires were in that casket when we opened it; diamonds, too, and rubies; amethysts, emeralds, pearls; all manner of precious stones," as likely as not the translator will say, "All precious stones were in that chest"; and where the author says, "Strange trees grew by the lake," as likely as not the translator will say, "Spanish moss hung from the branches of trees I did not know, not by their leaves nor by their bark could I tell what trees they were, and in the tops of some were mistletoe, and the roots of the mangroves went down into the lake."

III

As a literary curiosity I call to the reader's attention the poem *Le Guignon,* of which the translation is printed on page 49. If I am not mistaken, he will find the last two stanzas of this poem strangely familiar, and may even be able to place them at once as occurring in almost identical form in Thomas Gray's *Elegy Written in a Country Churchyard.* It is possible, also, that he will wonder what the *first* part of the poem reminds him of; it reminds him of a stanza from Longfellow's *Psalm of Life.* One day when I was looking at some photographs of drawings which Baudelaire made of himself and of his friends, I came across the facsimile of a sheet of scratch-paper covered with sketches and writing—two heads of a man, one of a woman, and two stanzas of verse in Baudelaire's hand. The upper stanza begins:

"Full many a gem of purest ray serene"

The lower stanza begins:

"Art is long, and time is fleeting"

In what appear to be some notes for Baudelaire's preface to the second edition of *Les Fleurs du Mal,* one finds this: "Note on plagiarisms.—Thomas Gray. Edgar Poe (2 passages). Longfellow (2 passages) . . ." One of the plagiarisms from Poe will be found on page 31, in the last line of *L'Héautontimorouménos:* "To laugh, but who can smile no more." Mr. Dillon has taken Baudelaire's line and translated it back into Poe.

In two of my translations, *Dawn* and *Parisian Dream,* I have used the French *rime riche,* which is in English not a rhyme at all. The French consider two words which are identical in sound and even identical in spelling, as rhyming, just because they are different in meaning. If English were French, the sentence, "I meant to buy two, too, when I was in Timbuktu," would furnish the four rhyming words for the octave of a sonnet. This sort of

rhyme, a rhyme for the mind, not for the ear, is practically unknown in English, although we often use as rhymes words like
"home," "come"; "blind," "wind," which are not ear-rhymes, but
partly eye-rhymes, partly mind-rhymes—the mind being dimly
aware that there was a time in our language when the vowel
sounds of "blind" and "wind" were identical.[1]

After having worked on French poetry all summer with the
greatest concentration and absorption, I found myself beginning to
use the *rime riche* quite naturally.

There are several passages in *Les Fleurs du Mal* so ambiguous
or so generally obscure that no one can say of them with certainty
that he is sure of their meaning. One of these passages occurs
in *Les Litanies de Satan*, and runs as follows:

> *Toi qui mets dans les yeux et dans le coeur des filles*
> *Le culte de la plaie et l'amour des guenilles,*

The literal translation of these lines presents few difficulties.
There is a possibility that the word *filles* is meant to be understood
as *jeunes filles* (young girls, maidens) ; but most people will concede that it is much more likely to stand for *filles publiques*
(prostitutes), and will accept the following as a literal rendering:
"Thou that dost put into the eyes and into the heart of prostitutes
the cult of the wound and the love of rags."

[1] The same thing can be said, I feel convinced, of "home" and "come".
But whereas I have authority for saying that the words "blind" and "wind"
once rhymed not only for the eye but also for the ear, I have not been able
to find so far any support of my assumption concerning "home" and "come".
I have only the following to offer, which seems to me suggestive: in the
country in Maine, where the descendants of the 17th century English
settlers still use the broad *a* of their ancestors, pronouncing "bath", "path",
"calf", etc., as the English do, and where many words and expressions now
obsolete in England are still in common use, I have often as a child heard
the word "home" pronounced "hum". *That Lucy Robbins—always a-gaddin',
never to hum!*

[xxvii]

But when once this is translated, how much wiser are you? What, if anything, does it mean? What *is* the "cult of the wound"? What sort of wound?—a bleeding wound?—a sore (implying disease)?—suffering in general? And whose wound?—whose suffering? One's own?—one's lover's?—the world's? Has "the cult of the wound" to do perhaps with the wounds of the crucified Christ? And if so, should the line be taken as suggesting a passionate and active sympathy on the part of harlots for the diseased and poor? Or is something far less innocent to be understood, something profoundly and diabolically blasphemous? At one period of my work on this poem I translated the phrase, "The cult of the stigmata."

Considering these two lines apart from their context, there would be little doubt, I think, in the mind of any reader, that they have erotic significance. The efficacy of blood, of the sight of bleeding wounds, as a stimulus to sexual ardour, is often indicated and sometimes broadly developed in the poetry of Baudelaire—as in *A celle qui est trop gai*, for instance; in *Une Martyre;* even, in a different sense, in *La Fontaine de Sang*.

If the meaning of "the cult of the wound" is to be found along this line, then what of "the love of rags"? How can these two expressions be brought into a logical relationship with each other? (Apparently they were very closely connected in the poet's mind: at one stage of its composition the second line of the couplet was in the form of "the love of the wound and a cult of rags".) Can "rags" be considered as "tawdry finery", "tinsel trappings", "rags and tags and velvet gowns"? Or can it be construed that these women, in addition to the pleasure which they derive from physical pain, from being flogged or cut, enjoy also dressing themselves in rags, as a symbol of abject servitude?

As I said, taken out of their context, these lines would seem plainly to have erotic significance. But by what are they preceded

[xxviii]

in the poem?—by a picture of the rich man, the "banker" (as Baudelaire has him in an earlier version), who is branded by Satan as "vile" and "without pity." "Do not", the poem might seem to be advising one, "do not, when you are down and out, when you are ragged, sick and starving in the streets of Paris, turn to the rich man, the banker, the respected, orderly member of society, the pillar of the Church, for help; these people in their hearts are vile and pitiless. Go rather to some common little street-walker; she it is who will firmly propel you to a marble-topped table and treat you to a *café crème* and a *brioche;* she it is who, if you have got into a scrape and the *flics* are after you, will hide you in an untidy closet and feed you on stale pastry until the affair has blown over."

It struck me that possibly the blasphemy hidden in this passage lay not so much in the suggestion of a fairly conventional sex-perversion, as in this jeering nudge in the very ribs of Christian society.

My translation of *Les Litanies de Satan* is to be found on page 115.

IV

Charles Baudelaire is the most widely-read poet in France today. One has only to talk with French publishers, with salesmen in bookshops in Paris, with the shabby, often erudite *bouquinistes,* unpadlocking their slant-roofed little book-stalls along the quays of the Seine, to realize that this is so. But why is it so? Is it something shocking, something lascivious about his poetry, is it the sensual pictures which he sometimes suggests to the imagination, that scratch the iron palate of the modern reader? I think it is not so much that, as that Baudelaire, with his cold intellect, his religion troubled by doubts and which he constantly affronted and blas-phemed, his mind that could not go mad, although, as he says,

[xxix]

equipped with all the machinery for going mad, his quiet facing of the facts that men are for the most part very stupid, that governments are bound to be corrupt, that Charles Baudelaire is destined to be a dinner for worms, that not all French writers are great writers, nor all German, English and American writers uncultured poetasters and barbarians—was our contemporary, was what we call a "modern"; except in those instances in which he is still in advance of us. He was, however, an aristocrat, and an individualist; [1] and since the trend of the present would seem to be away from the aristocrat and toward the proletariat, away from the individual and toward the mass, these attributes will serve to stamp him in the opinion of many people as, while not necessarily contemporaneous with his own generation, certainly outmoded today, certainly pre-War. The fact that throughout his life he loved the poor and sympathized with them, and that he was constantly accusing the rich of oppressing the poor, will seem merely paternalistic and charitable. Yet even those who will not admit at all in Baudelaire the quality of mind which I call "modern" cannot be unaware of the tremendous influence of his work on modern poetry, foreign as well as French. Philippe Soupault says,[2] "Indeed it is not exaggerated to write that French poetry in its entirety has been, for a period of thirty years, under the domination, more or less recognized, of *Les Fleurs du Mal.*"

Charles Baudelaire was a true Parisian, a poet of the city, a confirmed city-dweller. His pleasures were found in those amenities

1 Baudelaire's revolutionary activities, when in 1848 he published, together with two friends, a republican newspaper denouncing Louis-Philippe, and wore the white shirt of the revolutionist (always, according to Porché, immaculate and of the finest linen) were of short duration. He wrote later to Poulet-Malassis that the events of the revolution had thoroughly depoliticated him, and that he should thenceforth concern himself not at all with "*la polémique humaine.*"

2 *Baudelaire*, p. 54

which the city affords, and which can be found at their best only there: handsome architecture; exhibitions of paintings and etchings; shop-windows full of engravings and interesting bibelots; elegant ladies wearing furs and jewels and smelling of synthetic perfumes; the conversation of his peers; *Tannhäuser* played by a great orchestra. The New York skyline, with the tremendous Empire State building, with the sequined Chrysler tower silver in the sunlight, with the lights suddenly blazing like yellow sapphires in a million windows, above the outrageous, whirling, dining and conniving town—New York as a spectacle would have delighted him. (You have only to read his *Rêve Parisien* to see that there is some ground for what I say.)

This was a poet of the intellect, a lover of order, of perfection in form, deploring superstition, sentimentality and romanticism, feeling that one's life should be controlled by one's will, and that he had failed signally when his *Petits Poèmes en Prose,* although excellent in themselves, turned out to be something different from what he had proposed that they should be, having refused to subject themselves entirely to his intention and to his will. He says in a letter to Josephin Soulary: "I admired in the scheme of your poem your spirit of order, indispensable to the true poet."

Nature, in nearly all its manifestations, was abhorrent to him; Art was his god. Consider the following extract from a letter written to Fernand Desnoyers, in 1855: "My dear Desnoyers,—You ask me for some verses for your little volume, verses about *nature,* isn't that so?—about the woods, the great oaks, verdure, insects— the sun, no doubt? But you know very well that I am incapable of becoming sentimental over vegetation, and that my soul is rebellious to that singular new religion, which must always hold, it seems to me, for every *intellectual* being something rather *shocking.* I shall never believe that the soul of the Gods dwells in plants,

[xxxi]

and even if it did dwell there, I should be only moderately concerned, and I should consider my own as being of ever so much greater value than that of sanctified vegetables. I have always thought, even, that there was in flourishing and ever rejuvenated nature something distressing, something hard, cruel—an intangible something bordering upon effrontery."

It is by no means safe to believe every word that Baudelaire says, in his letters, or in his conversation. He loved to shock people, and did so on all sorts of occasions. It was one of the attributes, he held, of the elegant, reserved and sophisticated person, the "dandy," that he was always shocking other people while never on any occasion being shocked by anything himself. This letter on the subject of nature might easily have been written just to give a jolt to poor Desnoyers, who had innocently requested some verses about nature for his "little volume." But a brief consideration of Baudelaire's poetry, of his way of living, of what seem to have been his interests and pleasures will show that he is telling the truth; Baudelaire loved art, and he hated nature. "A person is perfectly well off anywhere," he wrote, "provided he is in good health, and has some books and engravings." And in speaking of the natural beauty of a woman he said, "What *is* this natural beauty, to compare with the ordered, planned perfection of a woman whose beauty has been determined by art, whose appearance, whose manner, have been consciously perfected in every detail, who has perfect control of her gesture as of her voice, who is never startled into expressing something she does not wish to express." (This is a paraphrase of the original.)

You will note that in his dream (*Rêve Parisien*) where he is painter and architect and can fashion everything to his liking, the first thing he does is to banish from the scene all vegetation, as being "irregular," and that the pools in this stately landscape are surrounded not by trees, but by colonnades. It is doubtful if he knew one tree from another or one flower from another. He often uses the word *arbre* and the word *fleur*, but if he ever mentions any particular kind of tree or flower, you may be pretty sure that he is doing so for reasons of rhyme (*rose* to rhyme with *chlorose* in *Le Soleil*, for instance; *renoncule* to rhyme with *crépuscule* in *Une Martyre*). He speaks in the poem *L'Invitation au Voyage* of having flowers in the room; but you will note that they are "les *plus rares* fleurs"; and also that their vegetable fragrance has to be mingled with the animal scent of ambergris before it begins to interest him.

Out of his strange and very unhappy mind Charles Baudelaire made poems of great beauty, on a variety of subjects, and in a variety of moods. His subject-matter was often, in itself, scandalous, blasphemous, revolting. He, even more than the reader is aware of it, was aware of this. He hated, even more than the reader does, the degenerate, the degraded, the deformed. I say purposely *de*-generate, *de*-graded, *de*-formed. He hated all that *de*bilitated, *de*feated, *de*stroyed the majesty of the human mind. It was with this particle that he was at war. He proposed to conquer ugliness by making beauty of it.

The title *Les Fleurs du Mal* is not adequately translated as *Flowers of Evil*. These poems are flowers of doubt, flowers of torture, flowers of grief, flowers of blasphemy, flowers of weakness, flowers of disgust; cemetery flowers, fertilized by the corruption of the ardent and well-cared-for flesh; flowers forced on the sterile bough of the mind's unblossomy decay.

To be unaware of this while reading *Les Fleurs du Mal* is to be insensitive to the contact of one of the proudest, most uncompromising, and most original of poetic talents. To be aware of this is to be enabled to give oneself over without resistance, with that sense of security which one feels only when in the presence of subtle and balanced minds, into the power of a great poet.

I am speaking, of course, of *Les Fleurs du Mal* as Baudelaire wrote them. Yet I hope that in the translations presented here, these French poems, shipwrecked into English and fitted out with borrowed clothes, have nevertheless not lost entirely their identity, will still be able to speak, though in a foreign tongue.

EDNA ST. VINCENT MILLAY

19, quai Voltaire, Paris
October, 1935

TABLE DES MATIÈRES

*

CONTENTS

*

[xxxvii]

[xxxviii]

[xxxix]

FLOWERS OF EVIL

LE LÉTHÉ

Viens sur mon cœur, âme cruelle et sourde,
Tigre adoré, monstre aux airs indolents;
Je veux longtemps plonger mes doigts tremblants
Dans l'épaisseur de ta crinière lourde;

Dans tes jupons remplis de ton parfum
Ensevelir ma tête endolorie,
Et respirer, comme une fleur flétrie,
Le doux relent de mon amour défunt.

Je veux dormir! dormir plutôt que vivre!
Dans un sommeil, douteux comme la mort,
J'étalerai mes baisers sans remord
Sur ton beau corps poli comme le cuivre.

Pour engloutir mes sanglots apaisés
Rien ne me vaut l'abîme de ta couche;
L'oubli puissant habite sur ta bouche,
Et le Léthé coule dans tes baisers.

[2]

LETHE

Come to my arms, cruel and sullen thing;
Indolent beast, come to my arms again,
For I would plunge my fingers in your mane
And be a long time unremembering—

And bury myself in you, and breathe your wild
Perfume remorselessly for one more hour:
And breathe again, as of a ruined flower,
The fragrance of the love you have defiled.

I long to sleep; I think that from a stark
Slumber like death I could awake the same
As I was once, and lavish without shame
Caresses upon your body, glowing and dark.

To drown my sorrow there is no abyss,
However deep, that can compare with your bed.
Forgetfulness has made its country your red
Mouth, and the flowing of Lethe is in your kiss.

A mon destin, désormais mon délice,
J'obéirai comme un prédestiné;
Martyr docile, innocent condamné,
Dont la ferveur attise le supplice,

Je sucerai, pour noyer ma rancœur,
Le népenthès et la bonne ciguë
Aux bouts charmants de cette gorge aiguë
Qui n'a jamais emprisonné de cœur.

My doom, henceforward, is my sole desire:
As martyrs, being demented in their zeal,
Shake with delightful spasms upon the wheel,
Implore the whip, or puff upon the fire,

So I implore you, fervently resigned!
Come; I would drink nepenthe and long rest
At the sweet points of this entrancing breast
Wherein no heart has ever been confined.

G. D.

LE FLACON

Il est de forts parfums pour qui toute matière
Est poreuse. On dirait qu'ils pénètrent le verre.
En ouvrant un coffret venu de l'orient
Dont la serrure grince et rechigne en criant,

Ou dans une maison déserte quelque armoire
Pleine de l'âcre odeur des temps, poudreuse et noire,
Parfois on trouve un vieux flacon qui se souvient,
D'où jaillit toute vive une âme qui revient.

Mille pensers dormaient, chrysalides funèbres,
Frémissant doucement dans les lourdes ténèbres,
Qui dégagent leur aile et prennent leur essor,
Teintés d'azur, glacés de rose, lamés d'or.

Voilà le souvenir enivrant qui voltige
Dans l'air troublé; les yeux se ferment; le Vertige
Saisit l'âme vaincue et la pousse à deux mains
Vers un gouffre obscurci de miasmes humains;

THE PERFUME FLASK

All matter becomes porous to certain scents; they pass
Through everything; it seems they even go through glass.
When opening some old trunk brought home from the far east,
That scolds, feeling the key turned and the lid released—

Some wardrobe, in a house long uninhabited,
Full of the powdery odours of moments that are dead—
At times, distinct as ever, an old flask will emit
Its perfume; and a soul comes back to live in it.

Dormant as chrysalids, a thousand thoughts that lie
In the thick shadows, pulsing imperceptibly,
Now stir, now struggle forth; now their cramped wings unfold,
Tinted with azure, lustred with rose, sheeted with gold!

Oh, memories, how you rise and soar, and hover there!
The eyes close; dizziness, in the moth-darkened air,
Seizes the drunken soul, and thrusts it toward the verge—
Where mistily all human miasmas float and merge—

Il la terrasse au bord d'un gouffre séculaire,
Où, Lazare odorant déchirant son suaire,
Se meut dans son réveil le cadavre spectral
D'un vieil amour ranci, charmant et sépulcral.

Ainsi, quand je serai perdu dans la mémoire
Des hommes, dans le coin d'une sinistre armoire
Quand on m'aura jeté, vieux flacon désolé,
Décrépit, poudreux, sale, abject, visqueux, fêlé,

Je serai ton cercueil, aimable pestilence!
Le témoin de ta force et de ta virulence,
Cher poison préparé par les anges! liqueur
Qui me ronge, ô la vie et la mort de mon cœur!

Of a primeval gulf; and drops it to the ground,
There, where, like Lazarus rising, his grave-clothes half unwound,
And odorous, a cadaver from its sleep has stirred:
An old and rancid love, charming and long-interred.

Thus, when I shall be lost from sight, thus when all men
Forget me, in the dark and dusty corner then
Of that most sinister cupboard where the living pile
The dead—when, an old flask, cracked, sticky, abject, vile,

I lie at length—still, still, sweet pestilence of my heart,
As to what power thou hast, how virulent thou art,
I shall bear witness; safe shall thy dear poison be!
Thou vitriol of the gods! thou death and life of me!

E. ST. V. M.

LE REVENANT

Comme les anges à l'œil fauve,
Je reviendrai dans ton alcôve
Et vers toi glisserai sans bruit
Avec les ombres de la nuit;

Et je te donnerai, ma brune,
Des baisers froids comme la lune
Et des caresses de serpent
Autour d'une fosse rampant.

Quand viendra le matin livide,
Tu trouveras ma place vide,
Où jusqu'au soir il fera froid.

Comme d'autres par la tendresse,
Sur ta vie et sur ta jeunesse,
Moi, je veux régner par l'effroi!

THE REVENANT

Like angels with bright savage eyes
I will come treading phantom-wise
Hither where thou art wont to sleep,
Amid the shadows hollow and deep.

And I will give thee, my dark one,
Kisses as icy as the moon,
Caresses as of snakes that crawl
In circles round a cistern's wall.

When morning shows its livid face
There will be no-one in my place,
And a strange cold will settle here.

Others, not knowing what thou art,
May think to reign upon thy heart
With tenderness: I trust to fear.

G. D.

[11]

LA VIE ANTÉRIEURE

J'ai longtemps habité sous de vastes portiques
Que les soleils marins teignaient de mille feux,
Et que leurs grands piliers, droits et majestueux,
Rendaient pareils, le soir, aux grottes basaltiques.

Les houles, en roulant les images des cieux,
Mêlaient d'une façon solennelle et mystique
Les tout-puissants accords de leur riche musique
Aux couleurs du couchant reflété par mes yeux.

C'est là que j'ai vécu dans les voluptés calmes,
Au milieu de l'azur, des vagues, des splendeurs
Et des esclaves nus, tout imprégnés d'odeurs,

Qui me rafraîchissaient le front avec des palmes,
Et dont l'unique soin était d'approfondir
Le secret douloureux qui me faisait languir.

MY FORMER LIFE

I can remember a country of long, high colonnades
Which mirrored in their pale marble the prismatic light
Cast from the bright sea billows in a thousand shades,
And which resembled a cave of fluted basalt by night.

The ocean, strewn with sliding images of the sky,
Would mingle in a mysterious and solemn way,
Under the wild brief sunsets, its tremendous cry
With the reflected colours of the ruined day.

There did I dwell in quiet luxury apart,
Amid the slowly changing hues of clouds and waves;
And there I was attended by two naked slaves

Who sometimes fanned me with great fronds on either side,
And whose sole task was to let sink into my heart
The dolorous and beautiful secret of which I died.

G. D.

L'AVERTISSEUR

Tout homme digne de ce nom
A dans le cœur un Serpent jaune,
Installé comme sur un trône,
Qui, s'il dit: "Je veux!" répond: "Non!"

Plonge tes yeux dans les yeux fixes
Des Satyresses ou des Nixes,
La Dent dit: "Pense à ton devoir!"

Fais des enfants, plante des arbres,
Polis des vers, sculpte des marbres,
La Dent dit: "Vivras-tu ce soir?"

Quoi qu'il ébauche ou qu'il espère,
L'homme ne vit pas un moment
Sans subir l'avertissement
De l'insupportable Vipère.

THE FANG

No man that's worthy of the name
But in his helpless heart alive
Harbours a yellow, talkative
Serpent, he cannot hush nor tame.

Gaze if you like into the eyes
Of dryads. . . . Just before you drown,
The Fang says, "You've a date in town."

Beget your children, plant your trees,
Chisel your marble, build your song. . . .
The Fang says, "Well,—it's not for long."

Hope—if you're hopeful—or despair;
Nothing's to hinder you; but hark!—
Always the hissing head is there,
The insupportable remark.

E. ST. V. M.

CAUSERIE

Vous êtes un beau ciel d'automne, clair et rose!
Mais la tristesse en moi monte comme la mer,
Et laisse, en refluant, sur ma lèvre morose
Le souvenir cuisant de son limon amer.

—Ta main se glisse en vain sur mon sein qui se pâme;
Ce qu'elle cherche, amie, est un lieu saccagé
Par la griffe et la dent féroce de la femme.
Ne cherchez plus mon cœur; les bêtes l'ont mangé.

Mon cœur est un palais flétri par la cohue;
On s'y soûle, on s'y tue, on s'y prend aux cheveux.
—Un parfum nage autour de votre gorge nue! . . .

O Beauté, dur fléau des âmes! tu le veux!
Avec tes yeux de feu, brillants comme des fêtes,
Calcine ces lambeaux qu'ont épargnés les bêtes!

EPISODE

You are a lovely, rosy, lucid autumn sky!
But sadness mounts upon me like a flooding sea,
And ebbs, and ebbing, leaves my lips morose and dry,
Smarting with salty ooze, bitter with memory.

—Useless to slide your hand like that along my breast;
That which it seeks, my dear, is plundered; it is slit
By the soft paw of woman, that clawed while it caressed.
Useless to hunt my heart; the beasts have eaten it.

My heart is like a palace where the mob has spat;
There they carouse, they seize each other's hair, they kill.
—Your breast is naked . . . what exotic scent is that? . . .

O Beauty, iron flail of souls, it is your will!
So be it! Eyes of fire, bright in the darkness there,
Burn up these strips of flesh the beasts saw fit to spare.

E. ST. V. M.

[17]

LE JET D'EAU

Tes beaux yeux sont las, pauvre amante!
Reste longtemps sans les rouvrir,
Dans cette pose nonchalante
Où t'a surprise le plaisir.
Dans la cour le jet d'eau qui jase
Et ne se tait ni nuit ni jour,
Entretient doucement l'extase
Où ce soir m'a plongé l'amour.

La gerbe épanouie
En mille fleurs,
Où Phœbé réjouie
Met ses couleurs,
Tombe comme une pluie
De larges pleurs.

Ainsi ton âme qu'incendie
L'éclair brûlant des voluptés
S'élance, rapide et hardie,
Vers les vastes cieux enchantés.

THE FOUNTAIN

Thine eyes are heavy. Let them close.
Lie without opening them. Lie
Still in the lovely thoughtless pose
Where pleasure found thee. The long cry
Of moonlit waters that caress
The evening, languorous as thou art,
Lives on: So does the tenderness
Love has awakened in my heart.

The fountain leaps and flowers
    In many roses,
Whereon the moonlight flares.
Their crystal petals, falling,
    Falling for ever,
Are changèd to bright tears.

Even thus thy spirit, briefly lit
With the strange lightnings of desire,
Once more into the infinite
Flings up its pure forgetful fire,

Puis, elle s'épanche, mourante,
En un flot de triste langueur,
Qui par une invisible pente
Descend jusqu'au fond de mon cœur.

La gerbe épanouie
En mille fleurs,
Où Phœbé réjouie
Met ses couleurs,
Tombe comme une pluie
De larges pleurs.

O toi, que la nuit rend si belle,
Qu'il m'est doux, penché vers tes seins,
D'écouter la plainte éternelle
Qui sanglote dans les bassins!
Lune, eau sonore, nuit bénie,
Arbres qui frissonez autour,
Votre pure mélancolie
Est le miroir de mon amour

La gerbe épanouie
En mille fleurs,
Où Phœbé réjouie
Met ses couleurs,
Tombe comme une pluie
De larges pleurs.

As if the dusty earth to flee—
And blossoms there, and breaks apart,
And falls, and flows invisibly
Into the deep night of my heart.

    The fountain leaps and flowers
        In many roses,
    Whereon the moonlight flares.
    Their crystal petals, falling,
        Falling for ever,
    Are changèd to bright tears.

O thou, so fair and so forlorn,
How sweet, my lips upon thy breast,
To hear within its marble urn
The water sobbing without rest.
O moon, loud water, lovely night,
O leaves where the soft winds upstart,
O wild and melancholy light,
Ye are the image of my heart.

    The fountain leaps and flowers
        In many roses,
    Whereon the moonlight flares.
    Their crystal petals, falling,
        Falling for ever,
    Are changèd to bright tears.

G. D.

LA CHEVELURE

O toison, moutonnant jusque sur l'encolure!
O boucles! O parfum chargé de nonchaloir!
Extase! Pour peupler ce soir l'alcôve obscure
Des souvenirs dormant dans cette chevelure,
Je la veux agiter dans l'air comme un mouchoir!

La langoureuse Asie et la brûlante Afrique,
Tout un monde lointain, absent, presque défunt,
Vit dans tes profondeurs, forêt aromatique!
Comme d'autres esprits voguent sur la musique,
Le mien, ô mon amour! nage sur ton parfum.

J'irai là-bas où l'arbre et l'homme, pleins de sève,
Se pâment longuement sous l'ardeur des climats;
Fortes tresses, soyez la houle qui m'enlève!
Tu contiens, mer d'ébène, un éblouissant rêve
De voiles, de rameurs, de flammes et de mâts:

THE FLEECE

O shadowy fleece that falls and curls upon those bare
Lithe shoulders! O rich perfume of forgetfulness!
O ecstasy! To loose upon the midnight air
The memories asleep in this tumultuous hair,
I long to rake it in my fingers, tress by tress!

Asia the languorous, the burning solitude
Of Africa—a whole world, distant, all but dead—
Survives in thy profundities, O odorous wood!
My soul, as other souls put forth on the deep flood
Of music, sails away upon thy scent instead.

There where the sap of life mounts hot in man and tree,
And lush desire untamed swoons in the torrid zone,
Undulant tresses, wild strong waves, oh, carry me!
Dream, like a dazzling sun, from out this ebony sea
Rises; and sails and banks of rowers propel me on.

Un port retentissant où mon âme peut boire
A grands flots le parfum, le son et la couleur;
Où les vaisseaux, glissant dans l'or et dans la moire,
Ouvrent leurs vastes bras pour embrasser la gloire
D'un ciel pur où frémit l'éternelle chaleur.

Je plongerai ma tête amoureuse d'ivresse
Dans ce noir océan où l'autre est enfermé;
Et mon esprit subtil que le roulis caresse
Saura vous retrouver, ô féconde paresse,
Infinis bercements du loisir embaumé!

Cheveux bleus, pavillon de ténèbres tendues,
Vous me rendez l'azur du ciel immense et rond;
Sur les bords duvetés de vos mèches tordues
Je m'enivre ardemment des senteurs confondues
De l'huile de coco, du musc et du goudron.

Longtemps! toujours! ma main dans ta crinière lourde
Sèmera le rubis, la perle et le saphir,
Afin qu'à mon désir tu ne sois jamais sourde!
N'es-tu pas l'oasis où je rêve, et la gourde
Où je hume à longs traits le vin du souvenir?

All the confusion, all the mingled colours, cries,
Smells of a busy port, upon my senses beat;
Where smoothly on the golden streakèd ripples flies
The barque, its arms outspread to gather in the skies,
Against whose glory trembles the unabating heat.

In this black ocean where the primal ocean roars,
Drunken, in love with drunkenness, I plunge and drown;
Over my dubious spirit the rolling tide outpours
Its peace—oh, fruitful indolence, upon thy shores,
Cradled in languor, let me drift and lay me down!

Blue hair, darkness made palpable, like the big tent
Of desert sky all glittering with many a star
Thou coverest me—oh, I am drugged as with the blent
Effluvia of a sleeping caravan, the scent
Of coco oil impregnated with musk and tar.

Fear not! Upon this savage mane for ever thy lord
Will sow pearls, sapphires, rubies, every stone that gleams,
To keep thee faithful! Art not thou the sycamored
Oasis whither my thoughts journey, and the dark gourd
Whereof I drink in long slow draughts the wine of dreams?

G. D.   E. ST. V. M.

REMORDS POSTHUME

Lorsque tu dormiras, ma belle ténébreuse,
Au fond d'un monument construit en marbre noir,
Et lorsque tu n'auras pour alcôve et manoir
Qu'un caveau pluvieux et qu'une fosse creuse;

Quand la pierre, opprimant ta poitrine peureuse
Et tes flancs qu'assouplit un charmant nonchaloir,
Empêchera ton cœur de battre et de vouloir,
Et tes pieds de courir leur course aventureuse,

Le tombeau, confident de mon rêve infini,
—Car le tombeau toujours comprendra le poète,—
Durant ces longues nuits d'où le somme est banni,

Te dira: "Que vous sert, courtisane imparfaite,
De n'avoir pas connu ce que pleurent les morts?"
—Et le ver rongera ta peau comme un remords.

REMORSE TOO LATE

My dark and lovely thing, when you at length lie dead,
And sleep beneath a slab of marble black as pitch;
And have, for perfumed alcove and seductive bed,
Only a rainy cavern and a hollow ditch;

When the oppressive stone upon your frightened breast
Lets settle all its weight, and on your supple thighs;
Restrains your heart from beating, flattens it to rest;
Bends down and binds your feet, so roving, so unwise;

The tomb, that knows me well and reads my dream aright,
(What poet but confides his secret to the tomb?)
Will say to you some day during that endless night,

"They fare but ill, vain courtesan, in this cold room,
Who bring here no warm memories of true love to keep!"
—And like remorse the worm will gnaw you in your sleep.

E. ST. V. M.

L'HÉAUTONTIMOROUMÉNOS

Je te frapperai sans colère
Et sans haine,—comme un boucher!
Comme Moïse le rocher,
—Et je ferai de ta paupière,

Pour abreuver mon Sahara,
Jaillir les eaux de la souffrance,
Mon désir gonflé d'espérance
Sur tes pleurs salés nagera

Comme un vaisseau qui prend le large,
Et dans mon cœur qu'ils soûleront
Tes chers sanglots retentiront
Comme un tambour qui bat la charge!

Ne suis-je pas un faux accord
Dans la divine symphonie,
Grâce à la vorace Ironie
Qui me secoue et qui me mord?

HEAUTON TIMOROUMENOS

I mean to strike you without hate,
As butchers do; as Moses did
The rock. From under either lid
Your tears will flow to inundate

This huge Sahara which is I.
My heart, insensible with pain,
Caught in that flood will live again:
Will care whether it live or die—

Will strive as in the salty sea,
Drunken with brine and all but drowned,
Yet driven onward by the sound
Of your wild sobbing endlessly!

For look—I am at war, my dear,
With the whole universe. I know
There is no medicine for my woe.
Believe me, it is called Despair.

Elle est dans ma voix, la criarde!
C'est tout mon sang, ce poison noir!
Je suis le sinistre miroir
Où la mégère se regarde.

Je suis la plaie et le couteau!
Je suis le soufflet et la joue!
Je suis les membres et la roue,
Et la victime et le bourreau!

Je suis de mon cœur le vampire,
—Un de ces grands abandonnés
Au rire éternel condamnés,
Et qui ne peuvent plus sourire!

It runs in all my veins. I pray:
It cries in all my words. I am
The very glass where what I damn
Leers and admires itself all day.

I am the wound—I am the knife
The deep wound scabbards; the outdrawn
Rack, and the writhing thereupon;
The lifeless, and the taker of life.

I murder what I most adore,
Laughing: I am indeed of those
Condemned for ever without repose
To laugh—but who can smile no more.

G. D.

SEMPER EADEM

"D'où vous vient, disiez-vous, cette tristesse étrange,
Montant comme la mer sur le roc noir et nu?"
—Quand notre cœur a fait une fois sa vendange,
Vivre est un mal! C'est un secret de tous connu,

Une douleur très simple et non mystérieuse,
Et, comme votre joie, éclatante pour tous.
Cessez donc de chercher, ô belle curieuse!
Et, bien que votre voix soit douce, taisez-vous!

Taisez-vous, ignorante! âme toujours ravie!
Bouche au rire enfantin! Plus encore que la Vie,
La Mort nous tient souvent par des liens subtils.

Laissez, laissez mon cœur s'enivrer d'un mensonge,
Plonger dans vos beaux yeux comme dans un beau songe,
Et sommeiller longtemps à l'ombre de vos cils!

SEMPER EADEM

"What in the world," you said, "has brought on this black mood,
Climbing you as the sea climbs up a naked reef?"
—When once the heart has made its harvest (understood
By all men, this) why, just to be alive is grief:

A pain quite simple, nothing mysterious at all,
And like that joy of yours, patent to all we meet;
Stop asking questions, then, I beg of you, and fall
Silent a while, fair prober, though your voice be sweet.

Ah, yes, be silent, ignorant girl, always so gay,
Mouth with the childlike laughter! More than Life, I say,
Death has the power to hold us by most subtle ties.

My one fictitious comfort, kindly, let me keep:
To plunge as into dreams into your lovely eyes,
And in the shadow of your lashes fall asleep.

E. ST. V. M.

LES HIBOUX

Sous les ifs noirs qui les abritent
Les hiboux se tiennent rangés,
Ainsi que des dieux étrangers,
Dardant leur œil rouge. Ils méditent.

Sans remuer ils se tiendront
Jusqu'à l'heure mélancolique
Où, poussant le soleil oblique,
Les ténèbres s'établiront.

Leur attitude au sage enseigne
Qu'il faut en ce monde qu'il craigne
Le tumulte et le mouvement;

L'homme ivre d'une ombre qui passe
Porte toujours le châtiment
D'avoir voulu changer de place.

THE OWLS

The owls that roost in the black yew
Along one limb in solemn state,
And with a red eye look you through,
Are eastern gods; they meditate.

No feather stirs on them, not one,
Until that melancholy hour
When night, supplanting the weak sun,
Resumes her interrupted power.

Their attitude instructs the wise
To shun all action, all surprise.
Suppose there passed a lovely face,—

Who even longs to follow it,
Must feel for ever the disgrace
Of having all but moved a bit.

                    E. ST. V. M.

L'HORLOGE

Horloge! dieu sinistre, effrayant, impassible,
Dont le doigt nous menace et nous dit: Souviens-toi!
Les vibrantes Douleurs dans ton cœur plein d'effroi
Se planteront bientôt comme dans une cible;

Le Plaisir vaporeux fuira vers l'horizon
Ainsi qu'une sylphide au fond de la coulisse;
Chaque instant te dévore un morceau du délice
A chaque homme accordé, pour toute sa saison.

Trois mille six cents fois par heure, la Seconde
Chuchote: Souviens-toi!—Rapide, avec sa voix
D'insecte, Maintenant dit: Je suis Autrefois,
Et j'ai pompé ta vie avec ma trompe immonde!

Remember! Souviens-toi! prodigue! Esto memor!
(Mon gosier de métal parle toutes les langues.)
Les minutes, mortel folâtre, sont des gangues
Qu'il ne faut pas lâcher sans en extraire l'or!

THE CLOCK

Terrible Clock! God without mercy; mighty Power!
Saying all day, "*Remember!* Remember and beware:
There is no arrow of pain but in a tiny hour
Will make thy heart its target, and stick and vibrate there.

"Toward the horizon all too soon and out of sight
Vaporous Pleasure, like a sylphide, floats away;
Each instant swallows up one crumb of that delight
Accorded to each man for all his mortal day."

The Second says, three thousand six hundred times an hour,
"*Remember!* Look, the wingèd insect Now doth sit
Upon thy vein, and shrilleth, 'I am Nevermore,
And I have sucked thy blood; I am flying away with it!'

"*Remember! Souviens-toi! Esto memor!*—no tongue
My metal larynx does not speak—O frivolous man,
These minutes, rich in gold, slide past; thou art not young;
Remember! and wash well the gravel in the pan!

Souviens-toi *que le Temps est un joueur avide*
Qui gagne sans tricher, à tout coup! c'est la loi.
Le jour décroît; la nuit augmente, souviens-toi!
Le gouffre a toujours soif; la clepsydre se vide.

Tantôt sonnera l'heure où le divin Hasard,
Où l'auguste Vertu, ton épouse encor vierge,
Où le Repentir même (oh! la dernière auberge!),
Où tout te dira: Meurs, vieux lâche! il est trop tard!"

"*Remember!* Time, the player that need not cheat to win,
Makes a strong adversary. Is thy game begun?
Thy game is lost! Day wanes; night waxes. Look within
The gulf,—it still is thirsty. The sands are all but run.

"Soon, soon, the hour will strike, when Hazard, he that showed
A god-like face, when Virtue—thy bride, but still intact—
When even Repentance (oh, last inn along the road!)
Will say to thee, 'Die, coward. It is too late to act.'"

E. ST. V. M.

DE PROFUNDIS CLAMAVI

J'implore ta pitié, Toi, l'unique que j'aime,
Du fond du gouffre obscur où mon cœur est tombé.
C'est un univers morne à l'horizon plombé,
Où nagent dans la nuit l'horreur et le blasphème;

Un soleil sans chaleur plane au-dessus six mois,
Et les six autres mois la nuit couvre la terre;
C'est un pays plus nu que la terre polaire;
Ni bêtes, ni ruisseaux, ni verdure, ni bois!

Or il n'est pas d'horreur au monde qui surpasse
La froide cruauté de ce soleil de glace
Et cette immense nuit semblable au vieux Chaos;

Je jalouse le sort des plus vils animaux
Qui peuvent se plonger dans un sommeil stupide,
Tant l'écheveau du temps lentement se dévide!

DE PROFUNDIS CLAMAVI

I do implore thy pity, Thou whom alone I love,
Deep in this mournful vale wherein my heart is fallen.
It is a world completely sad, where the low sullen
Skies seem about to rain pure horror from above.

A fireless sun swims over six months of every year;
Six months of every year the earth is lost in shadow.
It is a bleaker land than any Arctic meadow:
Nor streams, nor flowers, nor fruits, nor birds, nor forests here!

Surely there is no evil imaginable to compare
With the cruelty of that cold sun in the cold air
And that enormous night, like the first chaos of things;

I envy the very animals, to whom slumber brings
Over and over the gift of being thoughtless and blind,
So slowly does the thread of these dark years unwind.

G. D.

MÆSTA ET ERRABUNDA

Dis-moi, ton cœur parfois s'envole-t-il, Agathe,
Loin du noir océan de l'immonde cité,
Vers un autre océan où la splendeur éclate,
Bleu, clair, profond, ainsi que la virginité?
Dis-moi, ton cœur parfois s'envole-t-il, Agathe?

La mer, la vaste mer console nos labeurs!
Quel démon a doté la mer, rauque chanteuse
Qu'accompagne l'immense orgue des vents grondeurs,
De cette fonction sublime de berceuse?
La mer, la vaste mer console nos labeurs!

Emporte-moi, wagon! enlève-moi, frégate!
Loin! loin! ici la boue est faite de nos pleurs!
—Est-il vrai que parfois le triste cœur d'Agathe
Dise: Loin des remords, des crimes, des douleurs,
Emporte-moi, wagon, enlève-moi, frégate?

MÆSTA ET ERRABUNDA

Agatha, tell me, thy heart—does it sometimes fly away,
Far from the vast dark ocean of the mournful town,
Toward one still vaster, mirroring the blue, blue day,
Mindless and deep: a flood wherein all sorrows drown?
Agatha, tell me, thy heart—does it sometimes fly away?

The sea, the enormous sea has rest for our desires:
By what demoniac irony can that fierce thing,
That raucous howler to the winds' untuneful choirs,
Assuage our deepest woe with its wild clamouring?
The sea, the enormous sea has rest for our desires.

Carry me off, loud trains! Abstract me, silent ships,
Far, far! Here even the earth is miry with our tears!
Is it not true that sometimes Agatha's sweet lips
Murmur: "Far from regrets, from griefs, from cruel fears,
Carry me off, loud trains! Abstract me, silent ships!"

Comme vous êtes loin, paradis parfumé,
Où sous un clair azur tout n'est qu'amour et joie,
Où tout ce que l'on aime est digne d'être aimé,
Où dans la volupté pure le cœur se noie!
Comme vous êtes loin, paradis parfumé!

Mais le vert paradis des amours enfantines,
Les courses, les chansons, les baisers, les bouquets,
Les violons vibrant derrière les collines,
Avec les brocs de vin, le soir, dans les bosquets,
—Mais le vert paradis des amours enfantines,

L'innocent paradis, plein de plaisirs furtifs,
Est-il déjà plus loin que l'Inde ou que la Chine?
Peut-on le rappeler avec des cris plaintifs
Et l'animer encor d'une voix argentine,
L'innocent paradis plein de plaisirs furtifs?

How far, how far away, that paradise above,
Where all our ills supposedly are put to rest,
Where everything we love is worthy of our love,
And the unburdened heart lies weightless in the breast—
How far, how far away, that paradise above!

But the green, earthly paradise of childhood, even,
The songs, the furtive kisses, the dances, the bouquets,
The picnics on the hillside—that unpretentious heaven
Of summer twilights where a distant music plays:
But the green, earthly paradise of childhood, even,

Where all our cares are mended in small secret joys—
Is it already farther than Shanghai or Ceylon?
Or has the heart some kingdom no suffering destroys,
Where those young voices laugh, where those old tunes play on,
Where all our cares are mended in small secret joys?

G. D.

LE PORTRAIT

La Maladie et la Mort font des cendres
De tout le feu qui pour nous flamboya.
De ces grands yeux si fervents et si tendres,
De cette bouche où mon cœur se noya,

De ces baisers puissants comme un dictame,
De ces transports plus vifs que des rayons,
Que reste-t-il? C'est affreux, ô mon âme!
Rien qu'un dessin fort pâle, aux trois crayons,

Qui, comme moi, meurt dans la solitude,
Et que le Temps, injurieux vieillard,
Chaque jour frotte avec son aile rude . . .

Noir assassin de la Vie et de l'Art,
Tu ne tueras jamais dans ma mémoire
Celle qui fut mon plaisir et ma gloire!

THE PORTRAIT

Disease and Death, these are the ashes of
All that was fire, and warmed us heretofore.
Of those big eyes, so full of faith and love,
That mouth which stopped my heart, that endless store

Of kisses strong as dittany—that whole
Transport, that passion hotter than the sun,
What now remains? A sorry thing, my soul!
A faded sketch, in three pale crayons done;

Which, like myself, in dusty solitude
Subsides, and which with his injurious wing
Time daily rubs against. O black and rude

Assassin of proud Life and powerful Art:
You cannot rob my memory of one thing,—
Her, that was all my triumph, all my heart.

E. ST. V. M.

LE GUIGNON

Pour soulever un poids si lourd,
Sisyphe, il faudrait ton courage!
Bien qu'on ait du cœur à l'ouvrage,
L'Art est long et le Temps est court.

Loin des sépultures célèbres,
Vers un cimetière isolé,
Mon cœur, comme un tambour voilé,
Va battant des marches funèbres.

—Maint joyau dort enseveli
Dans les ténèbres et l'oubli,
Bien loin des pioches et des sondes;

Mainte fleur épanche à regret
Son parfum doux comme un secret
Dans les solitudes profondes.

ILL-STARRED

A man would needs be brave and strong
As Sisyphus, for such a task!
It is not greater zeal I ask—
But life is brief, and art is long.

To a forsaken mound of clay
Where no admirers ever come,
My heart, like an invisible drum,
Goes beating a dead march all day.

Many a jewel of untold worth
Lies slumbering at the core of earth,
In darkness and oblivion drowned;

Many a flower has bloomed and spent
The secret of its passionate scent
Upon the wilderness profound.

                                    G. D.

LA GÉANTE

Du temps que la Nature en sa verve puissante
Concevait chaque jour des enfants monstrueux,
J'eusse aimé vivre auprès d'une jeune géante,
Comme aux pieds d'une reine un chat voluptueux.

J'eusse aimé voir son corps fleurir avec son âme
Et grandir librement dans ses terribles jeux,
Deviner si son cœur couve une sombre flamme
Aux humides brouillards qui nagent dans ses yeux;

Parcourir à loisir ses magnifiques formes,
Ramper sur le versant de ses genoux énormes,
Et parfois en été, quand les soleils malsains,

Lasse, la font s'étendre à travers la campagne,
Dormir nonchalamment à l'ombre de ses seins,
Comme un hameau paisible au pied d'une montagne.

THE GIANTESS

In times of old when Nature in her glad excess
Brought forth such living marvels as no more are seen,
I should have loved to dwell with a young giantess,
Like a voluptuous cat about the feet of a queen;

To run and laugh beside her in her terrible games,
And see her grow each day to a more fearful size,
And see the flowering of her soul, and the first flames
Of passionate longing in the misty depths of her eyes;

To scale the slopes of her huge knees, explore at will
The hollows and the heights of her—and when, oppressed
By the long afternoons of summer, cloudless and still,

She would stretch out across the countryside to rest,
I should have loved to sleep in the shadow of her breast,
Quietly as a village nestling under a hill.

G. D.

RÊVE PARISIEN

I

De ce terrible paysage,
Que jamais œil mortel ne vit,
Ce matin encore l'image,
Vague et lointaine, me ravit.

Le sommeil est plein de miracles!
Par un caprice singulier,
J'avais banni de ces spectacles
Le végétal irrégulier,

Et, peintre fier de mon génie,
Je savourais dans mon tableau
L'enivrante monotonie
Du métal, du marbre et de l'eau.

Babel d'escaliers et d'arcades,
C'était un palais infini,
Plein de bassins et de cascades
Tombant dans l'or mat ou bruni;

PARISIAN DREAM

I

That marvellous landscape of my dream—
Which no eye knows, nor ever will—
At moments, wide awake, I seem
To grasp, and it excites me still.

Sleep, how miraculous you are—
A strange caprice had urged my hand
To banish, as irregular,
All vegetation from that land;

And, proud of what my art had done,
I viewed my painting, knew the great
Intoxicating monotone
Of marble, water, steel and slate.

Staircases and arcades there were
In a long labyrinth, which led
To a vast palace; fountains there
Were gushing gold, and gushing lead.

Et des cataractes pesantes,
Comme des rideaux de cristal,
Se suspendaient, éblouissantes,
A des murailles de métal.

Non d'arbres, mais de colonnades
Les étangs dormants s'entouraient,
Où de gigantesques naïades.
Comme des femmes, se miraient.

Des nappes d'eau s'épanchaient, bleues.
Entre des quais roses et verts,
Pendant des millions de lieues,
Vers les confins de l'univers;

C'étaient des pierres inouïes
Et des flots magiques; c'étaient
D'immenses glaces éblouies
Par tout ce qu'elles reflétaient!

Insouciants et taciturnes,
Des Ganges, dans le firmament,
Versaient le trésor de leurs urnes
Dans des gouffres des diamant.

And many a heavy cataract
Hung like a curtain,—did not fall,
As water does, but hung, compact,
Crystal, on many a metal wall.

Tall nymphs with Titan breasts and knees
Gazed at their images unblurred,
Where groves of colonnades, not trees,
Fringed a deep pool where nothing stirred.

Blue sheets of water, left and right,
Spread between quays of rose and green,
To the world's end and out of sight,
And still expanded, though unseen.

Enchanted rivers, those—with jade
And jasper were their banks bedecked;
Enormous mirrors, dazzled, made
Dizzy by all they did reflect.

And many a Ganges, taciturn
And heedless, in the vaulted air,
Poured out the treasure of its urn
Into a gulf of diamond there.

Architecte de mes féeries,
Je faisais, à ma volonté,
Sous un tunnel de pierreries,
Passer un océan dompté;

Et tout, même la couleur noire,
Semblait fourbi, clair, irisé;
Le liquide enchâssait sa gloire
Dans le rayon cristallisé.

Nul astre d'ailleurs, nuls vestiges
De soleil, même au bas du ciel,
Pour illuminer ces prodiges,
Qui brillaient d'un feu personnel!

Et sur ces mouvantes merveilles
Planait (terrible nouveauté!
Tout pour l'œil, rien pour les oreilles!)
Un silence d'éternité.

II

En rouvrant mes yeux pleins de flamme
J'ai vu l'horreur de mon taudis,
Et senti, rentrant dans mon âme,
La pointe des soucis maudits;

As architect, it tempted me
To tame the ocean at its source;
And this I did,—I made the sea
Under a jeweled culvert course.

And every colour, even black,
Became prismatic, polished, bright;
The liquid gave its glory back
Mounted in iridescent light.

There was no moon, there was no sun,—
For why should sun and moon conspire
To light such prodigies?—each one
Blazed with its own essential fire!

A silence like eternity
Prevailed, there was no sound to hear;
These marvels all were for the eye,
And there was nothing for the ear.

II

I woke; my mind was bright with flame;
I saw the cheap and sordid hole
I live in, and my cares all came
Burrowing back into my soul.

La pendule aux accents funèbres
Sonnait brutalement midi,
Et le ciel versait des ténèbres
Sur ce triste monde engourdi.

Brutally the twelve strokes of noon
Against my naked ear were hurled;
And a grey sky was drizzling down
Upon this sad, lethargic world.

E. ST. V. M.

LA FONTAINE DE SANG

Il me semble parfois que mon sang coule à flots,
Ainsi qu'une fontaine aux rythmiques sanglots.
Je l'entends bien qui coule avec un long murmure,
Mais je me tâte en vain pour trouver la blessure.

A travers la cité, comme dans un champ clos,
Il s'en va, transformant les pavés en îlots,
Désaltérant la soif de chaque créature,
Et partout colorant en rouge la nature.

J'ai demandé souvent à des vins captieux
D'endormir pour un jour la terreur qui me mine;
Le vin rend l'œil plus clair et l'oreille plus fine!

J'ai cherché dans l'amour un sommeil oublieux,
Mais l'amour n'est pour moi qu'un matelas d'aiguilles
Fait pour donner à boire à ces cruelles filles!

THE FOUNTAIN OF BLOOD

It seems to me sometimes my blood is bubbling out
As fountains do, in rhythmic sobs; I feel it spout
And lapse; I hear it plainly; it makes a murmuring sound;
But from what wound it wells, so far I have not found.

As blood runs in the lists, round tumbled armoured bones,
It soaks the city, islanding the paving-stones;
Everything thirsty leans to lap it, with stretched head;
Trees suck it up; it stains their trunks and branches red.

I turn to wine for respite, I drink, and I drink deep;
(Just for one day, one day, neither to see nor hear!)
Wine only renders sharper the frantic eye and ear.

In terror I cry to love, "Oh, put my mind to sleep!"
But love for me is only a mattress where I shrink
On needles, and my blood is given to whores to drink.

E. ST. V. M.

LE VAMPIRE

Toi qui, comme un coup de couteau,
Dans mon cœur plaintif es entrée;
Toi qui, forte comme un troupeau
De démons, vins, folle et parée,

De mon esprit humilié
Faire ton lit et ton domaine,
—Infâme à qui je suis lié
Comme le forçat à la chaîne,

Comme au jeu le joueur têtu,
Comme à la bouteille l'ivrogne,
Comme aux vermines la charogne,
—Maudite, maudite sois-tu!

J'ai prié le glaive rapide
De conquérir ma liberté,
Et j'ai dit au poison perfide
De secourir ma lâcheté.

THE VAMPIRE

Thou who abruptly as a knife
Didst come into my heart; thou who,
A demon horde into my life,
Didst enter, wildly dancing, through

The doorways of my sense unlatched
To make my spirit thy domain—
Harlot to whom I am attached
As convicts to the ball and chain,

As gamblers to the wheel's bright spell,
As drunkards to their raging thirst,
As corpses to their worms—accurst
Be thou! Oh, be thou damned to hell!

I have entreated the swift sword
To strike, that I at once be freed;
The poisoned phial I have implored
To plot with me a ruthless deed.

Hélas! le poison et le glaive
M'ont pris en dédain et m'ont dit:
"Tu n'es pas digne qu'on t'enlève
A ton esclavage maudit,

Imbécile!—de son empire
Si nos efforts te délivraient,
Tes baisers ressusciteraient
Le cadavre de ton vampire!"

Alas! the phial and the blade
Do cry aloud and laugh at me:
"Thou art not worthy of our aid;
Thou art not worthy to be free.

"Though one of us should be the tool
To save thee from thy wretched fate,
Thy kisses would resuscitate
The body of thy vampire, fool!"

G. D.

TU METTRAIS L'UNIVERS ENTIER
DANS TA RUELLE

Tu mettrais l'univers entier dans ta ruelle,
Femme impure! L'ennui rend ton âme cruelle.
Pour exercer tes dents à ce jeu singulier,
Il te faut chaque jour un cœur au râtelier.
Tes yeux, illuminés ainsi que des boutiques
Et des ifs flamboyants dans les fêtes publiques,
Usent insolemment d'un pouvoir emprunté,
Sans connaître jamais la loi de leur beauté.

Machine aveugle et sourde, en cruautés féconde!
Salutaire instrument, buveur du sang du monde,
Comment n'as-tu pas honte et comment n'as-tu pas
Devant tous les miroirs vu pâlir tes appas?
La grandeur de ce mal où tu te crois savante
Ne t'a donc jamais fait reculer d'épouvante,
Quand la nature, grande en ses desseins cachés,
De toi se sert, ô femme, ô reine des péchés,
—De toi, vil animal,—pour pétrir un génie?

O fangeuse grandeur! sublime ignominie!

YOU'D TAKE THE ENTIRE UNIVERSE
TO BED WITH YOU

You'd take the entire universe to bed with you,
I think, just out of boredom, you lecherous, idle shrew!
You need, to keep your teeth sound, exercise your jaws,
Daily, for dinner, some new heart between your paws!
Your eyes, all lighted up like shops, like public fairs,
How insolent they are!—as if their power were theirs
Indeed!—this borrowed power, this Beauty, you direct
And use, whose law, however, you do not suspect.

Unwholesome instrument for health, O deaf machine
And blind, fecund in tortures!—how is it you have not seen,
You drinker of the world's blood, your mirrored loveliness
Blench and recoil? how is it you feel no shame? confess:
Has never, then, this evil's very magnitude
Caused you to stagger?—you, who think yourself so shrewd
In evil?—seeing how Nature, patient and abstruse—
O Woman, Queen of Sins, Vile Animal,—has made use
Of you, to mould a genius?—employed you all this time?

O muddy grandeur!—ignominy ironic and sublime!

E. ST. V. M.

BOHÉMIENS EN VOYAGE

La tribu prophétique aux prunelles ardentes
Hier s'est mise en route, emportant ses petits
Sur son dos, ou livrant à leurs fiers appétits
Le trésor toujours prêt des mamelles pendantes.

Les hommes vont à pied sous leurs armes luisantes
Le long des chariots où les leurs sont blottis,
Promenant sur le ciel des yeux appesantis
Par le morne regret des chimères absentes.

Du fond de son réduit sablonneux, le grillon,
Les regardant passer, redouble sa chanson;
Cybèle, qui les aime, augmente ses verdures,

Fait couler le rocher et fleurir le désert
Devant ces voyageurs, pour lesquels est ouvert
L'empire familier des ténèbres futures.

THE GYPSIES

They set out yesterday, the tribe of ragged seers
With burning eyes—bearing their little ones in nests
Upon their backs, or giving them, to stop their tears,
The teats of inexhaustible and swarthy breasts.

The men walk shouldering their rifles silently
Beside the hooded wagons with bright tatters hung,
And peer into the sky, as if they hoped to see
Some old mirage that beckoned them when they were young.

No matter where they journey through the meagre land,
The cricket will sing louder from his lair of sand,
And Cybele, who loves them, will smile where they advance:

The desert will be fruitful, the arid rock will flow
Before the footsteps of these wayfarers, who go
Eternally into the lightless realm of chance.

G. D.

LA VOIX

Mon berceau s'adossait à la bibliothèque,
Babel sombre, où roman, science, fabliau,
Tout, la cendre latine et la poussière grecque,
Se mêlaient. J'étais haut comme un in-folio.
Deux voix me parlaient. L'une, insidieuse et ferme,
Disait: "La Terre est un gâteau plein de douceur;
Je puis (et ton plaisir serait alors sans terme!)
Te faire un appétit d'une égale grosseur."
Et l'autre: "Viens! oh! viens voyager dans les rêves
Au delà du possible, au delà du connu!"
Et celle-là chantait comme le vent des grèves,
Fantôme vagissant, on ne sait d'où venu,
Qui caresse l'oreille et cependant l'effraie.
Je te répondis: "Oui! douce voix!" C'est d'alors
Que date ce qu'on peut, hélas! nommer ma plaie
Et ma fatalité. Derrière les décors
De l'existence immense, au plus noir de l'abîme,
Je vois distinctement des mondes singuliers,
Et, de ma clairvoyance extatique victime,
Je traîne des serpents qui mordent mes souliers.
Et c'est depuis ce temps que, pareil aux prophètes,
J'aime si tendrement le désert et la mer;

THE VOICE

I grew up in the shadow of a big bookcase: a tall
Babel, where verses, novels, histories, row upon row—
The immemorial ashes of Greek and Latin—all
Mingled and murmured. When I was as high as a folio,
I heard two voices speaking. The first one said: "Be wise;
The world is but a large, delicious cake, my friend!
It calls for an appetite of corresponding size—
And whoso heeds my counsel, his joys shall have no end."
The other voice spoke softly: "Come, travel with me in dreams,
Far, far beyond the range of the possible and the known!"
And in that voice was the senseless music of winds and streams
Blown suddenly out of nowhere and into nowhere blown—
A phantom cry, a sound to frighten and captivate.
And I replied: "I will, O lovely voice!" And from
That hour was sealed for ever the disastrous fate
Which still attends me: Always, behind the tedium
Of finite semblances, beyond the accustomed zone
Of time and space, I see distinctly another world—
And I must wear with loathing these mortal toils, as one
Dragging a weight of serpents about his ankles curled.
And from that hour, like the old prophets of Palestine,
I love extravagantly the wilderness and the sea;

Que je ris dans les deuils et pleure dans les fêtes,
Et trouve un goût suave au vin le plus amer;
Que je prends très souvent les faits pour des mensonges
Et que, les yeux au ciel, je tombe dans des trous.
Mais la Voix me console et dit: "Garde tes songes;
Les sages n'en ont pas d'aussi beaux que les fous!"

I find an ineffable joy in the taste of harsh, sour wine;
I smile at the saddest moments; I weep amid gaiety;
I take facts for illusions—and often as not, with my eyes
Fixed confidently upon the heavens, I fall into holes.
But the Voice comforts me: "Guard, fool, thy dreams! The wise
Have none so beautiful as thou hast." And the Voice consoles.

G. D.

L'INVITATION AU VOYAGE

Mon enfant, ma sœur,
Songe à la douceur
D'aller là-bas vivre ensemble!
Aimer à loisir
Aimer et mourir
Au pays qui te ressemble!
Les soleils mouillés
De ces ciels brouillés
Pour mon esprit ont les charmes
Si mystérieux
De tes traîtres yeux,
Brillant à travers leurs larmes.

Là, tout n'est qu'ordre et beauté,
Luxe, calme et volupté.

Des meubles luisants,
Polis par les ans,
Décoreraient notre chambre;
Les plus rares fleurs
Mêlant leurs odeurs

INVITATION TO THE VOYAGE

Think, would it not be
Sweet to live with me
All alone, my child, my love?—
Sleep together, share
All things, in that fair
Country you remind me of?
Charming in the dawn
There, the half-withdrawn
Drenched, mysterious sun appears
In the curdled skies,
Treacherous as your eyes
Shining from behind their tears.

There, restraint and order bless
Luxury and voluptuousness.

We should have a room
Never out of bloom:
Tables polished by the palm
Of the vanished hours
Should reflect rare flowers

Aux vagues senteurs de l'ambre,
Les riches plafonds,
Les miroir profonds,
La splendeur orientale,
Tout y parlerait
A l'âme en secret
Sa douce langue natale.

Là, tout n'est qu'ordre et beauté,
Luxe, calme et volupté.

Vois sur ces canaux
Dormir ces vaisseaux
Dont l'humeur est vagabonde;
C'est pour assouvir
Ton moindre désir
Qu'ils viennent du bout du monde.
—Les soleils couchants
Revêtent les champs,
Les canaux, la ville entière,
D'hyacinthe et d'or;
Le monde s'endort
Dans une chaude lumière.

Là, tout n'est qu'ordre et beauté,
Luxe, calme et volupté.

In that amber-scented calm;
    Ceilings richly wrought,
    Mirrors deep as thought,
Walls with eastern splendour hung,—
    All should speak apart
    To the homesick heart
In its own dear native tongue.

There, restraint and order bless
Luxury and voluptuousness.

    See, their voyage past,
    To their moorings fast,
On the still canals asleep,
    These big ships; to bring
    You some trifling thing
They have braved the furious deep.
    —Now the sun goes down,
    Tinting dyke and town,
Field, canal, all things in sight,
    Hyacinth and gold;
    All that we behold
Slumbers in its ruddy light.

There, restraint and order bless
Luxury and voluptuousness.

E. ST. V. M.

[77]

QUE DIRAS-TU CE SOIR...

Que diras-tu ce soir, pauvre âme solitaire,
Que diras-tu, mon cœur, cœur autrefois flétri,
A la très belle, à la très bonne, à la très chère,
Dont le regard divin t'a soudain refleuri?

—Nous mettrons notre orgueil à chanter ses louanges,
Rien ne vaut la douceur de son autorité;
Sa chair spirituelle a le parfum des Anges,
Et son œil nous revêt d'un habit de clarté.

Que ce soit dans la nuit et dans la solitude,
Que ce soit dans la rue et dans la multitude,
Son fantôme dans l'air danse comme un flambeau.

Parfois il parle et dit: "Je suis belle, et j'ordonne
Que pour l'amour de moi vous n'aimiez que le Beau.
Je suis l'Ange gardien, la Muse et la Madone."

WHAT SHALL YOU SAY TONIGHT?

What shall you say tonight, poor soul so full of care,
What shall you say, my heart, heart hitherto so sad,
To the most kind, to the most dear, to the most fair,
Whose pure serene regard has made you proud and glad?

—We shall set all our pride to sing her holy praise!
What sweetness to be hers! To live beneath her sight!
Half spirit is her flesh, angelic all her ways;
Her glance alone invests us in a robe of light!

Whether in solitude and deep obscurity,
Whether by day among the moving crowd it be,
Her phantom like a torch in air will dance and run;

It speaks: "Beauty is mine; Authority is mine;
Love only, for my sake, the noble and the fine:
I am thine Angel, Muse, Madonna, all in one."

E. ST. V. M.

LA BÉATRICE

Dans des terrains cendreux, calcinés, sans verdure,
Comme je me plaignais un jour à la nature,
Et que de ma pensée, en vaguant au hasard,
J'aiguisais lentement sur mon cœur le poignard,
Je vis en plein midi descendre sur ma tête
Un nuage funèbre et gros d'une tempête,
Qui portait un troupeau de démons vicieux,
Semblables à des nains cruels et curieux.
A me considérer froidement ils se mirent,
Et, comme des passants sur un fou qu'ils admirent,
Je les entendis rire et chuchoter entre eux,
En échangeant maint signe et maint clignement d'yeux :

—"Contemplons à loisir cette caricature
Et cette ombre d'Hamlet imitant sa posture,
Le regard indécis et les cheveux au vent.
N'est-ce pas grand'pitié de voir ce bon vivant,
Ce gueux, cet histrion en vacances, ce drôle,
Parce qu'il sait jouer artistement son rôle,
Vouloir intéresser au chant de ses douleurs

BEATRICE

In a burned-over land, where not a blade or leaf
Showed green, through a charred world, whetting my ancient grief
Slowly upon my heart, and making sad lament
To Nature, at broad noon, not knowing where I went,
I walked . . . and saw above me a big cloud—which at first
I took to be a storm—blacken, and swell and burst,
And pour upon my head instead of rain a rout
Of demons, dwarfed and cruel, which ringed me all about.
As passers-by, no matter upon what errands bent,
Will always stop and stare with cold astonishment
At some poor man gone mad, then bait him wittily,
Just so they gaped and nudged, and jeered aloud at me.

—"Come! Have a look at this! What is it, should you say?
The shade of Hamlet—why, of course!—look at the way
He stands!—that undecided eye!—the wild hair, too!
Come here! Do look! Oh, wouldn't it wring a tear from you!
This shabby bon-vivant, this pompous tramp, this ham-
Actor out of a job, thinking that he can cram,
By ranting, stale gesticulations, crocodile-tears,

Les aigles, les grillons, les ruisseaux et les fleurs,
Et même à nous, auteurs de ces vieilles rubriques
Réciter en hurlant ses tirades publiques?"

J'aurais pu—mon orgueil aussi haut que les monts
Domine la nuée et le cri des démons!—
Détourner simplement ma tête souveraine,
Si je n'eusse pas vu parmi leur troupe obscène
—Crime qui n'a pas fait chanceler le soleil!—
La reine de mon cœur au regard nonpareil,
Qui riait avec eux de ma sombre détresse
Et leur versait parfois quelque sale caresse.

His tragic fate into the ears of crickets, into the ears
Of eagles!—yes, who knows?—along with brooks and flowers—
Forgetting we invented these tricks, even into ours!"

But for one thing—no mountain is taller than my pride;
No demon horde can scale me—I could have turned aside
My sovereign thought, and stood alone . . . had I not seen
Suddenly, amongst this loathsome troupe, *her*, my heart's queen—
And the sun did not reel, it stood unmoved above!—
Her of the pure deep gaze, my life, my peerless love,
Mocking and pointing, laughing at my acute distress;
Or fondling some foul dwarf in an obscene caress.

E. ST. V. M.

LES BIJOUX

La très chère était nue, et, connaissant mon cœur,
Elle n'avait gardé que ses bijoux sonores,
Dont le riche attirail lui donnait l'air vainqueur
Qu'ont dans leurs jours heureux les esclaves des Maures.

Quand il jette en dansant son bruit vif et moqueur,
Ce monde rayonnant de métal et de pierre
Me ravit en extase, et j'aime avec fureur
Les choses où le son se mêle à la lumière.

Elle était donc couchée, et se laissait aimer,
Et du haut du divan elle souriait d'aise
A mon amour profond et doux comme la mer
Qui vers elle montait comme vers sa falaise.

Les yeux fixés sur moi, comme un tigre dompté,
D'un air vague et rêveur elle essayait des poses,
Et la candeur unie à la lubricité
Donnait un charme neuf à ses métamorphoses.

THE JEWELS

The lovely one was naked and, knowing well my prayer,
She wore her loud bright armoury of jewels. They
Evoked in her the savage and victorious air
Of Moorish concubines upon a holiday.

When it gives forth, being shaken, its gay mocking noise,
This world of metal and of stone, aflare in the night,
Excites me monstrously, for chiefest of my joys
Is the luxurious commingling of sound and light.

Relaxed among the pillows, she looked down at me
And let herself be gazed upon at leisure—as if
Lulled by my wordless adoration, like the sea
Washing perpetually about the foot of a cliff.

Slowly, regarding me like a trained leopardess,
She slouched into successive poses. A certain ease,
A certain candour coupled with lasciviousness,
Lent a new charm to the old metamorphoses.

Et son bras et sa jambe, et sa cuisse et ses reins,
Polis comme de l'huile, onduleux comme un cygne,
Passaient devant mes yeux clairvoyants et sereins;
Et son ventre et ses seins, ces grappes de ma vigne,

S'avançaient plus câlins que les anges du mal,
Pour troubler le repos où mon âme était mise,
Et pour la déranger du rocher de cristal,
Où calme et solitaire elle s'était assise.

Je croyais voir unis par un nouveau dessin
Les hanches de l'Antiope au buste d'un imberbe,
Tant sa taille faisait ressortir son bassin.
Sur ce teint fauve et brun le fard était superbe!

—Et la lampe s'étant résignée à mourir,
Comme le foyer seul illuminait la chambre,
Chaque fois qu'il poussait un flamboyant soupir,
Il inondait de sang cette peau couleur d'ambre!

The whole lithe harmony of loins, hips, buttocks, thighs,
Tawny and sleek, and undulant as the neck of a swan,
Began to move hypnotically before my eyes:
And her large breasts, those fruits I have grown lean upon,

I saw float toward me, tempting as the angels of hell,
To win my soul in thraldom to their dark caprice
Once more, and lure it down from the high citadel
Where, calm and solitary, it thought to have found peace.

She stretched and reared, and made herself all belly. In truth,
It was as if some playful artist had joined the stout
Hips of Antiope to the torso of a youth! . . .
The room grew dark, the lamp having flickered and gone out,

And now the whispering fire that had begun to die,
Falling in lucent embers, was all the light therein—
And when it heaved at moments a flamboyant sigh
It inundated as with blood her amber skin.

G. D.

TOUT ENTIÈRE

Le *Démon*, dans ma chambre haute,
Ce matin est venu me voir,
Et, tâchant à me prendre en faute,
Me dit: *"Je voudrais bien savoir,*

Parmi toutes les belles choses
Dont est fait son enchantement,
Parmi les objets noirs ou roses
Qui composent son corps charmant,

Quel est le plus doux."—O mon âme,
Tu répondis à l'*Abhorré:*
"Puisqu'en elle tout est dictame,
Rien ne peut être préféré.

Lorsque tout me ravit, j'ignore
Si quelque chose me séduit.
Elle éblouit comme l'Aurore
Et console comme la Nuit;

ALL, ALL

The Devil up my attic stair
Came tiptoeing a while ago
And, trying to catch me unaware,
Said laughing, "I should like to know,

"Of all her many charms, what springs
Most often to your mind? Of all
The rose-coloured and shadowy things
Whereby her beauty may enthrall,

"Which is the sweetest?"—O my soul,
You answered the abhorrèd Guest:
"Her beauty is complete and whole.
No single part is loveliest.

"When she is near, I cannot say
What gives me such intense delight.
She dazzles like the break of day,
She comforts like the fall of night.

Et l'harmonie est trop exquise,
Qui gouverne tout son beau corps,
Pour que l'impuissante analyse
En note les nombreux accords.

O métamorphose mystique
De tous mes sens fondus en un!
Son haleine fait la musique,
Comme sa voix fait le parfum!"

"My senses seem to merge in one;
The harmony that rules her being
Is all my knowledge—I have none
Of hearing, smelling, touching, seeing.

"No, no. I cannot make a choice
In this sublime bewilderment.
Perhaps the music of her scent!
Perhaps the perfume of her voice!"

G. D.

LA SERVANTE AU GRAND CŒUR

La servante au grand cœur dont vous étiez jalouse,
Et qui dort son sommeil sous une humble pelouse,
Nous devrions pourtant lui porter quelques fleurs.
Les morts, les pauvres morts ont de grandes douleurs,
Et quand Octobre souffle, émondeur des vieux arbres,
Son vent mélancolique à l'entour de leurs marbres,
Certe, ils doivent trouver les vivants bien ingrats,
De dormir, comme ils font, chaudement dans leurs draps,
Tandis que, dévorés de noires songeries,
Sans compagnon de lit, sans bonnes causeries,
Vieux squelettes gelés travaillés par le ver,
Ils sentent s'égoutter les neiges de l'hiver
Et le siècle couler, sans qu'amis ni famille
Remplacent les lambeaux qui pendent à leur grille.

Lorsque la bûche siffle et chante, si le soir,
Calme, dans le fauteuil je la voyais s'asseoir,
Si, par une nuit bleue et froide de décembre,
Je la trouvais tapie en un coin de ma chambre,

THE OLD SERVANT

The servant that we had, you were so jealous of,
I think we might at least lay flowers on her grave.
Good creature, she's beneath the sod . . . and we're above;
The dead, poor things, what valid grievances they have!
And, when October comes, stripping the wood of leaves,
And round their marble slabs the wind of autumn grieves,
Surely, a living man must seem to the cold dead
Somewhat unfeeling, sound asleep in his warm bed,
While, gnawed by blacker dreams than any we have known—
Lovers, good conversation, every pleasure gone—
Old bones concerning which the worm has had his say,
They feel the heavy snows of winter drip away,
And years go by, and no-one from the sagging vase
Lifts the dried flowers to put fresh flowers in their place.

Some evening, when the whistling log begins to purr,
Supposing, in that chair, appeared the ghost of her;
Supposing, on some cold and blue December night,
I found her in my room, humble, half out of sight,

Grave, et venant du fond de son lit éternel
Couver l'enfant grandi de son œil maternel,
Que pourrais-je répondre à cette âme pieuse
Voyant tomber des pleurs de sa paupière creuse?

And thoughtful, having come from her eternal bed
To shield her grown-up child, to soothe his troubled head,
What could I find to say to the poor faithful soul,—
Seeing the tears beneath those sunken eyelids roll?

E. ST. V. M.

LESBOS

Mère des jeux latins et des voluptés grecques,
Lesbos, où les baisers languissants ou joyeux,
Chauds comme les soleils, frais comme les pastèques,
Font l'ornement des nuits et des jours glorieux,
—Mère des jeux latins et des voluptés grecques,

Lesbos, où les baisers sont comme les cascades
Qui se jettent sans peur dans les gouffres sans fonds
Et courent, sanglotant et gloussant par saccades,
—Orageux et secrets, fourmillants et profonds;
Lesbos, où les baisers sont comme les cascades!

Lesbos où les Phrynés l'une l'autre s'attirent,
Où jamais un soupir ne resta sans écho,
A l'égal de Paphos les étoiles t'admirent,
Et Vénus à bon droit peut jalouser Sapho!
—Lesbos où les Phrynés l'une l'autre s'attirent,

LESBOS

Mother of Latin revelry and of Greek delight,
Lesbos, whereof the kisses, disconsolate or gay,
Hot as the sun, or cool as melons plucked by night,
Beguile the unshadowed and the shadowed hours away;
Mother of Latin revelry and of Greek delight,

Lesbos, whereof the kisses are whirlpools and cascades
Journeying carelessly into a dark abyss:
So wild the sobbing and laughter among thy colonnades,
So secret, so profound, so stormy, every kiss!
Lesbos, whereof the kisses are whirlpools and cascades!

Lesbos, where the sweet slaves one to another yearn,
Where there is never a glance without an echoing sign;
Even as upon Cyprus the stars upon thee burn
With praise, and Cyprus' queen is envious of thine,
Lesbos, where the sweet slaves one to another yearn—

Lesbos, terre des nuits chaudes et langoureuses,
Qui font qu'à leurs miroirs, stérile volupté,
Les filles aux yeux creux, de leurs corps amoureuses,
Caressent les fruits mûrs de leur nubilité,
Lesbos, terre des nuits chaudes et langoureuses,

Laisse du vieux Platon se froncer l'œil austère;
Tu tires ton pardon de l'excès des baisers,
Reine du doux empire, aimable et noble terre,
Et des raffinements toujours inépuisés.
Laisse du vieux Platon se froncer l'œil austère.

Tu tires ton pardon de l'éternel martyre
Infligé sans relâche aux cœurs ambitieux
Qu'attire loin de nous le radieux sourire
Entrevu vaguement au bord des autres cieux;
Tu tires ton pardon de l'éternel martyre!

Qui des Dieux osera, Lesbos, être ton juge,
Et condamner ton front pâli dans les travaux,
Si ses balances d'or n'ont pesé le déluge
De larmes qu'à la mer ont versé tes ruisseaux?
Qui des Dieux osera, Lesbos, être ton juge?

Lesbos, of sultry twilights and pure, infertile joy,
Where deep-eyed maidens, thoughtlessly disrobing, see
Their beauty, and are entranced before their mirrors, and toy
Fondly with the soft fruits of their nubility;
Lesbos, of sultry twilights and pure, infertile joy!

Let frown the old lined forehead of Plato as it will:
Thy pardon is assured—even by the strange excess,
Luxurious isle, of thy long sterile rapture, still
Contriving some new freak or form of tenderness;
Let frown the old lined forehead of Plato as it will.

Thy pardon has been bought with our eternal pain,
The lonely martyrdom endured in every age
By those who sigh for pleasures outlandish and insane
To ease the unearthly longing no pleasure can assuage.
Thy pardon has been bought with our eternal pain.

Who, Lesbos, of the gods would dare pronounce thy fate
And brand thy passionate white brow with infamy—
Or hope by any art or science to estimate
The tears, the tears thy streams have poured into the sea?
Who, Lesbos, of the gods would dare pronounce thy fate?

Que nous veulent les lois du juste et de l'injuste?
Vierges au cœur sublime, honneur de l'archipel,
Votre religion comme une autre est auguste,
Et l'amour se rira de l'enfer et du ciel!
—Que nous veulent les lois du juste et de l'injuste?

Car Lesbos entre tous m'a choisi sur la terre
Pour chanter le secret de ses vierges en fleur,
Et je fus dès l'enfance admis au noir mystère
Des rires effrénés mêlés au sombre pleur;
Car Lesbos entre tous m'a choisi sur la terre,

Et depuis lors je veille au sommet de Leucate,
Comme une sentinelle, à l'œil perçant et sûr,
Qui guette nuit et jour brick, tartane ou frégate,
Dont les formes au loin frissonnent dans l'azur,
—Et depuis lors je veille au sommet de Leucate

Pour savoir si la mer est indulgente et bonne,
Et parmi les sanglots dont le roc retentit
Un soir ramènera vers Lesbos qui pardonne
Le cadavre adoré de Sapho qui partit
Pour savoir si la mer est indulgente et bonne!

What are men's laws to us, injurious or benign?
Proud virgins, glory of the Ægean! We know well
Love, be it most foredoomed, most desperate, is divine,
And love will always laugh at heaven and at hell!
What are men's laws to us, injurious or benign?

Lo! I was named by Lesbos of all the lists of earth
To celebrate her sad-eyed girls and their sweet lore:
And I have known from childhood the noise of loud, crazed mirth
Confused mysteriously with terrible weeping—for
Lo! I was named by Lesbos of all the lists of earth.

And I have watched thenceforward from the Leucadian cliff,
Like an unwearying old sentry, who can descry
Far out on the horizon a sailboat or a skiff
Invisible to others, with his sharp, practised eye;
And I have watched thenceforward from the Leucadian cliff

To find if the cold wave were pitiful and good—
And someday I shall see come wandering home, I know,
To all-forgiving Lesbos upon the twilight flood
The sacred ruins of Sappho, who set forth long ago
To find if the cold wave were pitiful and good;

De la mâle Sapho, l'amante et le poète,
Plus belle que Vénus par ses mornes pâleurs!
—L'œil d'azur est vaincu par l'œil noir que tachette
Le cercle ténébreux tracé par les douleurs
De la mâle Sapho, l'amante et le poète!

—Plus belle que Vénus se dressant sur le monde
Et versant les trésors de sa sérénité
Et le rayonnement de sa jeunesse blonde
Sur le vieil Océan de sa fille enchanté;
Plus belle que Vénus se dressant sur le monde!

—De Sapho qui mourut le jour de son blasphème,
Quand, insultant le rite et le culte inventé,
Elle fit son beau corps la pâture suprême
D'un brutal dont l'orgueil punit l'impiété
De Sapho qui mourut le jour de son blasphème.

Et c'est depuis ce temps que Lesbos se lamente,
Et, malgré les honneurs que lui rend l'univers.
S'enivre chaque nuit du cri de la tourmente
Que poussent vers les cieux ses rivages déserts.
Et c'est depuis ce temps que Lesbos se lamente!

Of Sappho, poet and lover—the virile, calm, and brave,
More beautiful than Venus, by force of earthly grief—
More beautiful than blue-eyed Venus, with her grave
And dusky glance disclosing the sorrows past belief
Of Sappho, poet and lover—the virile, calm, and brave:

More beautiful than Venus arising to the world
And scattering all round her the iridescent fire
Of her blond loveliness with rainbow hues impearled
Upon the old green ocean, her bedazzled sire;
More beautiful than Venus arising to the world!

—Of Sappho, who died proudly the day of her soul's crime
When, faithless to her teaching and to her serious pledge,
She flung the occult dark roses of her love sublime
To a vain churl. Alas! How deep the sacrilege
Of Sappho, who died proudly the day of her soul's crime!

And from that day to this the isle of Lesbos mourns—
And heedful of the world's late homage in no wise,
Gives answer but with the hollow moaning of her wild bourns:
The sea's long obloquy to the unlistening skies!
And from that day to this the isle of Lesbos mourns.

G. D.

LA LUNE OFFENSÉE

O Lune qu'adoraient discrètement nos pères,
Du haut des pays bleus où, radieux sérail,
Les astres vont te suivre en pimpant attirail,
Ma vieille Cynthia, lampe de nos repaires,

Vois-tu les amoureux sur leurs grabats prospères,
De leur bouche en dormant montrer le frais émail?
Le poète buter du front sur son travail?
Ou sous les gazons secs s'accoupler les vipères?

Sous ton domino jaune, et d'un pied clandestin,
Vas-tu, comme jadis, du soir jusqu'au matin,
Baiser d'Endymion les grâces surannées?

"—Je vois ta mère, enfant de ce siècle appauvri,
Qui vers son miroir penche un lourd amas d'années,
Et plâtre artistement le sein qui t'a nourri!"

THE OUTRAGED MOON

O Moon, adored of old, discreetly, by our sires!
From that blue land above, where, in a glittering train,
Sandaled with gold, revealed through veils of gossamer rain,
The stars attend your steps and wait on your desires,

Do you, by chance, my ancient Cynthia, behold
The parted lips of lovers drowsy with delight?
Or, coupling under the dry grass, the writhing cold
Snakes? Or some poet working far into the night?

Or, shall we say, 'tis your old flame Endymion
Whose superannuated charms you gaze upon?
Fancy your keeping up that faded rendezvous!

—"Insolent child of this degenerate century,
Your wrinkled, simpering mother,—that is what I see.
Enamelling with art the breast that suckled you!"

E. ST. V. M.

BIEN LOIN D'ICI

C'est ici la case sacrée
Où cette fille très parée,
Tranquille et toujours préparée,

D'une main éventant ses seins,
Et son coude dans les coussins,
Écoute pleurer les bassins:

C'est la chambre de Dorothée.
—La brise et l'eau chantent au loin
Leur chanson de sanglots heurtée
Pour bercer cette enfant gâtée.

Du haut en bas, avec grand soin,
Sa peau délicate est frottée
D'huile odorante et de benjoin.
—Des fleurs se pâment dans un coin.

EVER SO FAR FROM HERE

This is the house, the sacred box,
Where, always draped in languorous frocks,
And always at home if someone knocks,

One elbow into the pillow pressed,
She lies, and lazily fans her breast,
While fountains weep their soulfullest:

This is the chamber of Dorothy.
—Fountain and breeze for her alone
Sob in that soothing undertone.
Was ever so spoiled a harlot known?

With odorous oils and rosemary,
Benzoin and every unguent grown,
Her skin is rubbed most delicately.
—The flowers are faint with ecstasy.

E. ST. V. M.

LE REBELLE

Un Ange furieux fond du ciel comme un aigle,
Du mécréant saisit à plein poing les cheveux,
Et dit, le secouant: "Tu connaîtras la règle!
(Car je suis ton bon Ange, entends-tu?) Je le veux!

Sache qu'il faut aimer, sans faire la grimace,
Le pauvre, le méchant, le tortu, l'hébété,
Pour que tu puisses faire à Jésus, quand il passe,
Un tapis triomphal avec ta charité.

Tel est L'Amour! Avant que ton cœur ne se blase,
A la gloire de Dieu rallume ton extase;
C'est la Volupté vraie aux durable appas!"

Et l'Ange, châtiant autant, ma foi! qu'il aime,
De ses poings de géant torture l'anathème;
Mais le damné répond toujours: "Je ne veux pas!"

THE REBEL

Falling abruptly like a bird of prey from the sky,
A furious angel seizes the sinner by his hair
And says, "I will teach you to behave, do you hear me? I
Am your good spirit!" And shakes him angrily in the air.

"I will teach you to be kind—to love, without making a face,
The poor, the deformed, the depraved, the uncivil, the dirty, the dumb,
That you may help with your charity to prepare a place
Here upon earth for Jesus when he is ready to come.

"Such is true love—the only virtue that exists,
The only happiness that endures. Take heed, before
Your heart is completely petrified and your senses rot."

And pounding upon his victim with his colossal fists
In love and in fury, the angel cannot cease to implore—
Nor the accursèd one to answer: "I will not!"

G. D.

[109]

CHATIMENT DE L'ORGUEIL

En ces temps merveilleux où la Théologie
Fleurit avec le plus de sève et d'énergie,
On raconte qu'un jour un docteur des plus grands
—Après avoir forcé les cœurs indifférents,
Les avoir remués dans leurs profondeurs noires;
Après avoir franchi vers les célestes gloires
Des chemins singuliers à lui-même inconnus,
Où les purs Esprits seuls peut-être étaient venus,
—Comme un homme monté trop haut, pris de panique,
S'écria, transporté d'un orgueil satanique:
"Jésus, petit Jésus! je t'ai poussé bien haut!
Mais, si j'avais voulu t'attaquer au défaut
De l'armure, ta honte égalerait ta gloire,
Et tu ne serais plus qu'un fœtus dérisoire!"

Immédiatement sa raison s'en alla.
L'éclat de ce soleil d'un crêpe se voila;
Tout le chaos roula dans cette intelligence,
Temple autrefois vivant, plein d'ordre et d'opulence,
Sous les plafonds duquel tant de pompe avait lui.
Le silence et la nuit s'installèrent en lui,
Comme dans un caveau dont la clef est perdue.

THE PUNISHMENT OF PRIDE

Once in that marvellous and unremembered time
When theologic thought was flowering at its prime,
A pious metaphysician, the pundit of his day,
He who could move the hearts of murderers, so they say,
Having attained to a most fearful pitch of grace
By curious pathways he himself could scarcely trace,
For all his subtlety of logic—this austere
And venerable person (like one who climbs a sheer
Peak unperturbed, but at the top grows dizzy) cried,
Suddenly overtaken with satanic pride:
"Jesus, my little Jesus! I have exalted you
Into a very Titan—yet wielding as I do
The wand of dialectic, I could have made you shrink
To foetus-like proportions and fade away, I think!"

He thought no more, for instantly his reason cracked.
The noontide of this great intelligence was blacked
Out. Elemental chaos rolled through this serene
Temple, where so much order and opulence had been.
From its gold floor to its groined ceiling it grew dim:
Silence and utter night installed themselves in him,
As in an antique dungeon whereof the key is lost.

Dès lors il fut semblable aux bêtes de la rue,
Et, quand il s'en allait sans rien voir, à travers
Les champs, sans distinguer les étés des hivers,
Sale, inutile et laid comme une chose usée,
Il faisait des enfants la joie et la risée.

And from that day, through rain and snow, through sleet and frost,
Not knowing spring from winter and too mad to care,
He roamed about gesticulating, with the air
Of an old suit of underclothes hung out to dry,
And made the children laugh whenever he went by.

G. D.

LES LITANIES DE SATAN

O toi, le plus savant et le plus beau des Anges,
Dieu trahi par le sort et privé de louanges,

O Satan, prends pitié de ma longue misère!

O Prince de l'exil, à qui l'on a fait tort,
Et qui, vaincu, toujours te redresses plus fort,

O Satan, prends pitié de ma longue misère!

Toi qui sais tout, grand roi des choses souterraines,
Guérisseur familier des angoisses humaines,

O Satan, prends pitié de ma longue misère!

Toi qui, même aux lépreux, aux parias maudits,
Enseignes par l'amour le goût du Paradis,

O Satan, prends pitié de ma longue misère!

THE LITANIES OF SATAN

O thou, of all the Angels loveliest and most learned,
To whom no praise is chanted and no incense burned,

Satan, have pity upon me in my deep distress!

O Prince of exile, god betrayed by foulest wrong,
Thou that in vain art vanquished, rising up more strong,

Satan, have pity upon me in my deep distress!

O thou who knowest all, each weak and shameful thing,
Kind minister to man in anguish, mighty king,

Satan, have pity upon me in my deep distress!

Thou that dost teach the leper, the pariah we despise,
To love like other men, and taste sweet Paradise,

Satan, have pity upon me in my deep distress!

[115]

O toi, qui de la Mort, ta vieille et forte amante,
Engendras l'Espérance,—une folle charmante!

O Satan, prends pitié de ma longue misère!

Toi qui fais au proscrit ce regard calme et haut
Qui damne tout un peuple autour d'un échafaud,

O Satan, prends pitié de ma longue misère!

Toi qui sais en quel coin des terres envieuses
Le Dieu jaloux cacha les pierres précieuses,

O Satan, prends pitié de ma longue misère!

Toi dont l'œil clair connaît les profonds arsenaux
Où dort enseveli le peuple des métaux,

O Satan, prends pitié de ma longue misère!

Toi dont la large main cache les précipices
Au somnambule errant au bord des édifices,

O Satan, prends pitié de ma longue misère!

O thou, that in the womb of Death, thy fecund mate,
Engenderest Hope, with her sweet eyes and her mad gait,

Satan, have pity upon me in my deep distress!

Thou who upon the scaffold dost give that calm and proud
Demeanour to the felon, which condemns the crowd,

Satan, have pity upon me in my deep distress!

Thou that hast seen in darkness and canst bring to light
The gems a jealous God has hidden from our sight,

Satan, have pity upon me in my deep distress!

Thou to whom all the secret arsenals are known
Where iron, where gold and silver, slumber, locked in stone,

Satan, have pity upon me in my deep distress!

Thou whose broad hand dost hide the precipice from him
Who, barefoot, in his sleep, walks on the building's rim,

Satan, have pity upon me in my deep distress!

Toi qui, magiquement, assouplis les vieux os
De l'ivrogne attardé foulé par les chevaux,

O Satan, prends pitié de ma longue misère!

Toi qui, pour consoler l'homme frêle qui souffre,
Nous appris à mêler le salpêtre et le soufre,

O Satan, prends pitié de ma longue misère!

Toi qui poses ta marque, ô complice subtil,
Sur le front du Crésus impitoyable et vil,

O Satan, prends pitié de ma longue misère!

Toi qui mets dans les yeux et dans le cœur des filles
Le culte de la plaie et l'amour des guenilles,

O Satan, prends pitié de ma longue misère!

Bâton des exilés, lampe des inventeurs,
Confesseur des pendus et des conspirateurs,

O Satan, prends pitié de ma longue misère!

O thou who makest supple between the horses' feet
The old bones of the drunkard fallen in the street,

Satan, have pity upon me in my deep distress!

Thou who hast taught the frail and over-burdened mind
How easily saltpeter and sulphur are combined,

Satan, have pity upon me in my deep distress!

Thou that hast burned thy brand beyond all help secure,
Into the rich man's brow, who tramples on the poor,

Satan, have pity upon me in my deep distress!

O thou, who makest gentle the eyes and hearts of whores
With kindness for the wretched, homage for rags and sores,

Satan, have pity upon me in my deep distress!

Staff of the exile, lamp of the inventor, last
Priest of the man about whose neck the rope is passed,

Satan, have pity upon me in my deep distress!

Père adoptif de ceux qu'en sa noire colère
Du paradis terrestre a chassés Dieu le Père,

O Satan, prends pitié de ma longue misère!

PRIÈRE

Gloire et louange à toi, Satan, dans les hauteurs
Du Ciel, où tu régnas, et dans les profondeurs
De l'Enfer où, vaincu, tu rêves en silence!
Fais que mon âme un jour, sous l'Arbre de Science,
Près de toi se repose, à l'heure où sur ton front
Comme un Temple nouveau ses rameaux s'épandront!

O thou, adopted father of those fatherless
Whom God from Eden thrust in terror and nakedness,

Satan, have pity upon me in my deep distress!

Glory and praise to thee, Satan, in the most high,
Where thou didst reign; and in deep hell's obscurity,
Where, manacled, thou broodest long! O silent power,
Grant that my soul be near to thee in thy great hour,
When, like a living Temple, victorious bough on bough,
Shall rise the Tree of Knowledge, whose roots are in thy brow!

E. ST. V. M.

TRISTESSES DE LA LUNE

Ce soir, la lune rêve avec plus de paresse;
Ainsi qu'une beauté, sur de nombreux coussins,
Qui d'une main distraite et légère caresse,
Avant de s'endormir, le contour de ses seins,

Sur le dos satiné des molles avalanches,
Mourante, elle se livre aux longues pâmoisons,
Et promène ses yeux sur les visions blanches
Que montent dans l'azur comme des floraisons.

Quand parfois sur ce globe, en sa langueur oisive,
Elle laisse filer une larme furtive,
Un poète pieux, ennemi du sommeil,

Dans le creux de sa main prend cette larme pâle,
Aux reflets irisés comme un fragment d'opale,
Et la met dans son cœur loin des yeux du soleil.

THE SADNESS OF THE MOON

Tonight the moon, by languorous memories obsessed,
Lies pensive and awake: a sleepless beauty amid
The tossed and multitudinous cushions of her bed,
Caressing with an abstracted hand the curve of her breast.

Surrendered to her deep sadness as to a lover, for hours
She lolls in the bright luxurious disarray of the sky—
Haggard, entranced—and watches the small clouds float by.
Uncurling indolently in the blue air like flowers.

When now and then upon this planet she lets fall,
Out of her idleness and sorrow, a secret tear,
Some poet—an enemy of slumber, musing apart—

Catches in his cupped hands the unearthly tribute, all
Fiery and iridescent like an opal's sphere,
And hides it from the sun for ever in his heart.

G. D.

LE JEU

Dans des fauteuils fanés des courtisanes vieilles,
Pâles, le sourcil peint, l'œil câlin et fatal,
Minaudant, et faisant de leurs maigres oreilles
Tomber un cliquetis de pierre et de métal;

Autour des verts tapis des visages sans lèvre,
Des lèvres sans couleur, des mâchoires sans dent,
Et des doigts convulsés d'une infernale fièvre,
Fouillant la poche vide ou le sein palpitant;

Sous de sales plafonds un rang de pâles lustres
Et d'énormes quinquets projetant leurs lueurs
Sur des fronts ténébreux de poètes illustres
Qui viennent gaspiller leurs sanglantes sueurs:

—Voilà le noir tableau qu'en un rêve nocturne
Je vis se dérouler sous mon œil clairvoyant,
Moi-même, dans un coin de l'antre taciturne,
Je me vis accoudé, froid, muet, enviant,

THE GAMING ROOM

The armchairs of worn satin; the aged courtesans,
Livid and rouged, their eyes relentless, their eyebrows blacked,
Jingling eternally from their withered ears, to attract
Attention, their huge ear-rings, and ogling behind their fans;

The long green table, the rows of lipless faces, the lips
Drained of all colour; the gaping, toothless mouths; the unrest
Of hundreds of white nervous fingers, stacking the chips,
Or searching the empty pocket, the convulsive breast;

The dirty ceiling, the blaze of crystal chandeliers,
The low-hung lamps illumining with a crude glare
The ravaged brows of poets, the scars of grenadiers,
Who come to risk the earnings of their life-blood there.

—Such is the lurid spectacle that with calm dread
I saw as in a melancholy dream unroll:
Myself, too, sitting in a deserted corner, my head
Propped in my hands, mute, weary, jealous to my soul,

Enviant de ces gens la passion tenace,
De ces vieilles putains la funèbre gaîté,
Et tous gaillardement trafiquant à ma face,
L'un de son vieil honneur, l'autre de sa beauté!

Et mon cœur s'effraya d'envier maint pauvre homme
Courant avec ferveur à l'abîme béant,
Et qui, soûl de son sang, préférerait en somme
La douleur à la mort et l'enfer au néant!

Jealous of all that rabble, of the lust of it,
The terrible gaiety of those old whores, the smell
And noise of life, for which they frantically sell
Some remnant of their honour, their beauty, or their wit.

And suddenly I was affrighted at my own heart, to feel
Such envy of all men running wildly and out of breath
Nowhere, and who prefer, like those around that wheel,
Pain, horror, crime, insanity—anything—to death!

G. D.

LA MUSE VÉNALE

O Muse de mon cœur, amante des palais,
Auras-tu, quand Janvier lâchera ses Borées,
Durant les noirs ennuis des neigeuses soirées,
Un tison pour chauffer tes deux pieds violets?

Ranimeras-tu donc tes épaules marbrées
Aux nocturnes rayons qui percent les volets?
Sentant ta bourse à sec autant que ton palais,
Récolteras-tu l'or des voûtes azurées?

Il te faut, pour gagner ton pain de chaque soir,
Comme un enfant de chœur, jouer de l'encensoir,
Chanter des Te Deum auxquels tu ne crois guère,

Ou, saltimbanque à jeun, étaler tes appas
Et ton rire trempé de pleurs qu'on ne voit pas,
Pour faire épanouir la rate du vulgaire.

THE MERCENARY MUSE

Muse of my heart, so fond of palaces, reply:
When January sends those blizzards wild and white,
Shall you have any fire at all to huddle by,
Chafing your violet feet in the black snowy night?

Think: when the moon shines through the window, shall you try
To thaw your marble shoulders in her square of light?
Think: when your purse is empty and your palate dry,
Can you from the starred heaven snatch all the gold in sight?

No, no; if you would earn your bread, you have no choice
But to become a choir-boy, and chant in a loud voice
Te Deums you have no faith in, and swing your censer high;

Or be a mountebank, employing all your art—
Yes, on an empty stomach and with an anguished heart—
To chase the boredom of the liverish gallery.

E. ST. V. M.

L'EXAMEN DE MINUIT

La pendule, sonnant minuit,
Ironiquement nous engage
A nous rappeler quel usage
Nous fîmes du jour qui s'enfuit:
—Aujourd'hui, date fatidique,
Vendredi, treize, nous avons,
Malgré tout ce que nous savons,
Mené le train d'un hérétique.

Nous avons blasphémé Jésus,
Des Dieux le plus incontestable!
Comme un parasite à la table
De quelque monstrueux Crésus,
Nous avons, pour plaire à la brute,
Digne vassale des Démons,
Insulté ce que nous aimons
Et flatté ce qui nous rebute;

AT MIDNIGHT

Ironic as the voice of Fate,
Those dulcet chimes will have us **start**
Pondering over, to our woe,
The ruined hours they bid depart.
Today was an unlucky date—
Friday, the thirteenth. O my heart,
In spite of everything we know,
How we have erred and fallen low!

We have offended Jesus, most
Admirable of gods by far:
Even as sycophants approve
Anything to be popular
Or please some vile and powerful **host**
(Creature of Satan that we are!)
We have insulted what we love,
Flattered what we have horror of—

Contristé, servile bourreau,
Le faible qu'à tort on méprise;
Salué l'énorme Bêtise,
La Bêtise au front de taureau;
Baisé la stupide Matière
Avec grande dévotion,
Et de la putréfaction
Béni la blafarde lumière.

Enfin, nous avons, pour noyer
Le vertige dans le délire,
Nous, prêtre orgueilleux de la Lyre,
Dont la gloire est de déployer
L'ivresse des choses funèbres,
But sans soif et mangé sans faim! . . .
—Vite, soufflons la lampe, afin
De nous cacher dans les ténèbres!

Heard falsehood, seen injustice done,
Helped to cry down the poor man's cause;
Paid homage to expressionless
Cold Matter; hailed with wild huzzas
Stupidity, that bull-like one
Whose very bigness overawes;
Nor have we been averse to bless
The pale glitter of putridness.

Finally, to cheat sadness, we
Have revelled at the board of Greed,
With neither thirst nor appetite—
We, of the old Pierian breed,
Whose pride was to win ecstasy
From sorrow, loneliness, and need.
—Hurry! Let us put out the light,
That we be hidden in the night.

G. D.

L'IMPRÉVU

Harpagon, qui veillait son père agonisant,
Se dit, rêveur, devant ces lèvres déjà blanches:
"Nous avons au grenier un nombre suffisant,
    Ce me semble, de vieilles planches?"

Célimène roucoule et dit: "Mon cœur est bon,
Et naturellement, Dieu m'a faite très belle."
—Son cœur! cœur racorni, fumé comme un jambon,
    Recuit à la flamme éternelle!

Un gazetier fumeux, qui se croit un flambeau,
Dit au pauvre, qu'il a noyé dans les ténèbres:
"Où donc l'aperçois-tu, ce créateur du Beau,
    Ce Redresseur que tu célèbres?"

Mieux que tous, je connais certain voluptueux
Qui bâille nuit et jour, et se lamente et pleure,
Répétant, l'impuissant et le fat: "Oui, je veux
    Être vertueux, dans une heure!"

THE UNFORESEEN

Harpagon, sitting up beside his father's bed,
Mused, as the breathing altered and the lips went grey,
"I've plenty of old planks, I think, out in the shed;
  I saw them there the other day."

Célimène coos and says, "How beautiful I am!
God, since my heart is kind, has made me fair, as well!"
Her heart!—as tough as leather, her heart!—smoked like a ham;
  And turning on a spit in hell!

A sputtering gazetteer, who thinks he casts a light,
Says to his readers drowned in paradox and doubt,
"Where do you see him, then, this God of Truth and Right?
  This Saviour that you talk about?"

Better than these I know—although I know all three—
That foppish libertine, who yawns in easy grief
Nightly upon my shoulder, "All right, you wait and see;
  I'm turning over a new leaf!"

L'horloge, à son tour, dit à voix basse: *"Il est mûr,*
Le damné! J'avertis en vain la chair infecte.
L'homme est aveugle, sourd, fragile, comme un mur
     Qu'habite et que ronge un insecte!"

Et puis, Quelqu'un paraît, que tous avaient nié,
Et qui leur dit, railleur et fier: *"Dans mon ciboire,*
Vous avez, que je crois, assez communié,
     A la joyeuse Messe noire?

Chacun de vous m'a fait un temple dans son cœur;
Vous avez, en secret, baisé ma fesse immonde!
Reconnaissez Satan à son rire vainqueur,
     Énorme et laid comme le monde!

Avez-vous donc pu croire, hypocrites surpris,
Qu'on se moque du maître, et qu'avec lui l'on triche,
Et qu'il soit naturel de recevoir deux prix,
     D'aller au Ciel et d'être riche?

Il faut que le gibier paye le vieux chasseur
Qui se morfond longtemps à l'affût de la proie.
Je vais vous emporter à travers l'épaisseur,
     Compagnons de ma triste joie,

The clock says, "The condemned is ready; you may call
For him; I have advised in vain as to those flaws
Which threatened; Man is blind, deaf, fragile—like a wall
   In which an insect lives and gnaws."

Whereat a Presence, stranger to few, greeted by none,
Appears. "Well met!" he mocks; "have I not seen you pass
Before my sacred vessel, in communion
   Of joyousness, at the Black Mass?

"Each of you builds in secret a temple to my fame;
Each one of you in secret has kissed my foul behind;
Look at me; hear this laughter: *Satan* is my name,—
   Lewd, monstrous as the world! Oh, blind,

"Oh, hypocritical men!—and did you think indeed
To mock your master?—trick him till double wage be given?
Did it seem likely two such prizes be decreed:
   To be so rich—and enter Heaven?

"The game must pay the hunter; the hunter for his prey
Lies chilled and cramped so long behind the vain decoy;
Down through the thickness now I carry you away,
   Companions of my dreary joy;

A travers l'épaisseur de la terre et du roc,
A travers les amas confus de votre cendre,
Dans un palais aussi grand que moi, d'un seul bloc,
    Et qui n'est pas de pierre tendre;

Car il est fait avec l'universel Péché,
Et contient mon orgueil, ma douleur et ma gloire!
—Cependant, tout en haut de l'univers juché,
    Un Ange sonne la victoire

De ceux dont le cœur dit: "Que béni soit ton fouet,
Seigneur! que la douleur, ô Père, soit bénie!
Mon âme dans tes mains n'est pas un vain jouet,
    Et ta prudence est infinie."

Le son de la trompette est si délicieux,
Dans ces soirs solennels de célestes vendanges,
Qu'il s'infiltre comme une extase dans tous ceux
    Dont elle chante les louanges.

"Down through the thickness of primeval earth and rock,
Thickness of human ashes helter-skelter blown,
Into a palace huge as I,—a single block—
    And of no soft and crumbling stone!—

"For it is fashioned whole from Universal Sin;
And it contains my grief, my glory and my pride!"
—Meantime, from his high perch above our earthly din,
    An Angel sounds the victory wide

Of those whose heart says, "Blessèd be this punishment,
O Lord! O Heavenly Father, be this anguish blest!
My soul in Thy kind hands at last is well content,
    A toy no more; Thou knowest best!"

So sweetly, so deliciously that music flows
Through the cool harvest evenings of these celestial days,
That like an ecstasy it penetrates all those
    Of whose pure lives it sings the praise.

E. ST. V. M.

LES CHATS

Les amoureux fervents et les savants austères
Aiment également dans leur mûre saison,
Les chats puissants et doux, orgueil de la maison,
Qui comme eux sont frileux et comme eux sédentaires.

Amis de la science et de la volupté,
Ils cherchent le silence et l'horreur des ténèbres;
L'Érèbe les eût pris pour ses coursiers funèbres,
S'ils pouvaient au servage incliner leur fierté.

Ils prennent en songeant les nobles attitudes
Des grands sphinx allongés au fond des solitudes,
Qui semblent s'endormir dans un rêve sans fin;

Leurs reins féconds sont pleins d'étincelles magiques,
Et des parcelles d'or, ainsi qu'un sable fin,
Étoilent vaguement leurs prunelles mystiques.

CATS

No-one but indefatigable lovers and old
Chilly philosophers can understand the true
Charm of these animals serene and potent, who
Likewise are sedentary and suffer from the cold.

They are the friends of learning and of sexual bliss;
Silence they love, and darkness where temptation breeds.
Erebus would have made them his funereal steeds,
Save that their proud free nature would not stoop to this.

Like those great sphinxes lounging through eternity
In noble attitudes upon the desert sand,
They gaze incuriously at nothing, calm and wise.

Their fecund loins give forth electric flashes, and
Thousands of golden particles drift ceaselessly,
Like galaxies of stars, in their mysterious eyes.

G. D.

À CELLE QUI EST TROP GAIE

Ta tête, ton geste, ton air
Sont beaux comme un beau paysage;
Le rire joue en ton visage
Comme un vent frais dans un ciel clair.

Le passant chagrin que tu frôles
Est ébloui par la santé
Qui jaillit comme une clarté
De tes bras et de tes épaules.

Les retentissantes couleurs
Dont tu parsèmes tes toilettes
Jettent dans l'esprit des poètes
L'image d'un ballet de fleurs.

Ces robes folles sont l'emblème
De ton esprit bariolé;
Folle dont je suis affolé,
Je te hais autant que je t'aime!

A GIRL TOO GAY

Oh, you are lovely! Every heart
Surrenders to your sorceries;
And laughter, like a playful breeze,
Is always blowing your lips apart.

Your health is radiant, infinite,
Superb: When you go down the street
Each mournful passer-by you meet
Is dazzled by the blaze of it!

Your startling dresses, overwrought
With rainbow hues and sequined showers,
Bring to a poet's mind the thought
Of a ballet of drunken flowers.

They are the very symbol of
Your gay and crudely coloured soul,
As stripèd as a barber's pole,
Exuberant thing I hate and love!

Quelquefois dans un beau jardin,
Où je traînais mon atonie,
J'ai senti comme une ironie
Le soleil déchirer mon sein ;

Et le printemps et la verdure
Ont tant humilié mon cœur
Que j'ai puni sur une fleur
L'insolence de la nature.

Ainsi, je voudrais, une nuit,
Quand l'heure des voluptés sonne,
Vers les trésors de ta personne
Comme un lâche ramper sans bruit,

Pour châtier ta chair joyeuse,
Pour meurtrir ton sein pardonné,
Et faire à ton flanc étonné
Une blessure large et creuse,

Et, vertigineuse douceur !
A travers ces lèvres nouvelles,
Plus éclatantes et plus belles,
T'infuser mon venin, ma sœur !

Sometimes when wandering, full of **gloom,**
In a bright garden, I have felt
Horror for all I touched and smelt:
The world outrageously in bloom,

The blinding yellow sun, the spring's
Raw verdure so rebuked my woes
That I have punished upon a rose
The insolence of flowering things.

Likewise, some evening, I would creep,
When midnight sounds, and everywhere
The sighing of lovers fills the air,
To the hushed alcove where you sleep,

And waken you by violent storm,
And beat you coldly till you swooned,
And carve upon your perfect form,
With care, a deep seductive wound—

And (joy delirious and complete!)
Through those bright novel lips, through this
Gaudy and virgin orifice,
Infuse you with my venom, sweet.

                                        G. D.

L'ALBATROS

Souvent, pour s'amuser, les hommes d'équipage
Prennent des albatros, vastes oiseaux des mers,
Qui suivent, indolents compagnons de voyage,
Le navire glissant sur les gouffres amers.

A peine les ont-ils déposés sur les planches,
Que ces rois de l'azur, maladroits et honteux,
Laissent piteusement leurs grandes ailes blanches
Comme des avirons traîner à côté d'eux.

Ce voyageur ailé, comme il est gauche et veule!
Lui, naguère si beau, qu'il est comique et laid!
L'un agace son bec avec un brûle-gueule,
L'autre mime, en boitant, l'infirme qui volait!

Le Poète est semblable au prince des nuées
Qui hante la tempête et se rit de l'archer;
Exilé sur le sol au milieu des huées,
Ses ailes de géant l'empêchent de marcher.

THE ALBATROSS

Sometimes, to entertain themselves, the men of the crew
Lure upon deck an unlucky albatross, one of those vast
Birds of the sea that follow unwearied the voyage through,
Flying in slow and elegant circles above the mast.

No sooner have they disentangled him from their nets
Than this aërial colossus, shorn of his pride,
Goes hobbling pitiably across the planks and lets
His great wings hang like heavy, useless oars at his side.

How droll is the poor floundering creature, how limp and weak—
He, but a moment past so lordly, flying in state!
They tease him: One of them tries to stick a pipe in his beak;
Another mimics with laughter his odd lurching gait.

The Poet is like that wild inheritor of the cloud,
A rider of storms, above the range of arrows and slings;
Exiled on earth, at bay amid the jeering crowd,
He cannot walk for his unmanageable wings.

G. D.

SPLEEN [I]

Pluviôse, irrité contre la vie entière,
De son urne à grands flots verse un froid ténébreux
Aux pâles habitants du voisin cimetière
Et la mortalité sur les faubourgs brumeux.

Mon chat sur le carreau cherchant une litière
Agite sans repos son corps maigre et galeux;
L'âme d'un vieux poète erre dans la gouttière
Avec la triste voix d'un fantôme frileux.

Le bourdon se lamente, et la bûche enfumée
Accompagne en fausset la pendule enrhumée,
Cependant qu'en un jeu plein de sales parfums,

Héritage fatal d'une vieille hydropique,
Le beau valet de cœur et la dame de pique
Causent sinistrement de leurs amours défunts.

LATE JANUARY

Pluviose, hating all that lives, and loathing me,
Distills his cold and gloomy rain and slops it down
Upon the pallid lodgers in the cemetery
Next door, and on the people shopping in the town.

My cat, for sheer discomfort, waves a sparsely-furred
And shabby tail incessantly on the tiled floor;
And, wandering sadly in the rain-spout, can be heard
The voice of some dead poet who had these rooms before.

The log is wet, and smokes; its hissing high lament
Mounts to the bronchial clock on the cracked mantel there;
While (heaven knows whose they were—some dropsical old maid's)

In a soiled pack of cards that reeks of dirty scent,
The handsome jack of hearts and the worn queen of spades
Talk in suggestive tones of their old love-affair.

E. ST. V. M.

SPLEEN [II]

J'ai plus de souvenirs que si j'avais mille ans.

Un gros meuble à tiroirs encombré de bilans,
De vers, de billets doux, de procès, de romances,
Avec de lourds cheveux roulés dans des quittances,
Cache moins de secrets que mon triste cerveau.
C'est une pyramide, un immense caveau,
Qui contient plus de morts que la fosse commune.
—Je suis un cimetière abhorré de la lune,
Où comme des remords se traînent de longs vers
Qui s'acharnent toujours sur mes morts les plus chers.
Je suis un vieux boudoir plein de roses fanées,
Où gît tout un fouillis de modes surannées,
Où les pastels plaintifs et les pâles Boucher,
Seuls, respirent l'odeur d'un flacon débouché.

Rien n'égale en longueur les boiteuses journées,
Quand sous les lourds flocons des neigeuses années
L'ennui, fruit de la morne incuriosité,
Prend les proportions de l'immortalité.

THE SPHINX

I swear to you that if I lived a thousand years
I could not be more crammed with dubious souvenirs.

There's no old chest of drawers bulging with deeds and bills,
Love-letters, locks of hair, novels, bad verses, wills,
That hides so many secrets as my wretched head;—
It's like a mausoleum, like a pyramid,
Holding more heaped unpleasant bones than Potter's Field;
I am a graveyard hated by the moon; revealed
Never by her blue light are those long worms that force
Into my dearest dead their blunt snouts of remorse.
—I am an old boudoir, where roses dried and brown
Have given their dusty odour to the faded gown,
To the ridiculous hat, doubtless in other days
So fine, among the wan pastels and pale Bouchers.

Time has gone lame, and limps; and under a thick pall
Of snow the endless years efface and muffle all;
Till boredom, fruit of the mind's inert, incurious tree,
Assumes the shape and size of immortality.

—*Désormais tu n'es plus, ô matière vivante!*
Qu'un granit entouré d'une vague épouvante,
Assoupi dans le fond d'un Saharah brumeux!
Un vieux sphinx ignoré du monde insoucieux,
Oublié sur la carte, et dont l'humeur farouche
Ne chante qu'aux rayons du soleil qui se couche.

Henceforth, O living matter, you are nothing more
Than the fixed heart of chaos, soft horror's granite core,
Than a forgotten Sphinx that in some desert stands,
Drowsing beneath the heat, half-hidden by the sands,
Unmarked on any map,—whose rude and sullen frown
Lights up a moment only when the sun goes down.

E. ST. V. M.

SPLEEN [III]

Je suis comme le roi d'un pays pluvieux,
Riche, mais impuissant, jeune et pourtant très vieux,
Qui, de ses précepteurs méprisant les courbettes,
S'ennuie avec ses chiens comme avec d'autres bêtes.
Rien ne peut l'égayer, ni gibier, ni faucon,
Ni son peuple mourant en face du balcon,
Du bouffon favori la grotesque ballade
Ne distrait plus le front de ce cruel malade;
Son lit fleurdelisé se transforme en tombeau,
Et les dames d'atour, pour qui tout prince est beau,
Ne savent plus trouver d'impudique toilette
Pour tirer un souris de ce jeune squelette.
Le savant qui lui fait de l'or n'a jamais pu
De son être extirper l'élément corrompu,
Et dans ces bains de sang qui des Romains nous viennent
Et dont sur leurs vieux jours les puissants se souviennent
Il n'a su réchauffer ce cadavre hébété
Où coule au lieu de sang l'eau verte du Léthé.

THE KING OF THE RAINY COUNTRY

A rainy country this, that I am monarch of,—
A rich but powerless king, worn-out while yet a boy;
For whom in vain the falcon falls upon the dove;
Not even his starving people's groans can give him joy;
Scorning his tutors, loathing his spaniels, finding stale
His favourite jester's quips, yawning at the droll tale.
His bed, for all its *fleurs de lis*, looks like a tomb;
The ladies of the court, attending him, to whom
He, being a prince, is handsome, see him lying there
Cold as a corpse, and lift their shoulders in despair:
No garment they take off, no garter they leave on
Excites the gloomy eye of this young skeleton.
The royal alchemist, who makes him gold from lead,
The baser element from out the royal head
Cannot extract; nor can those Roman baths of blood,
For some so efficacious, cure the hebetude
Of him, along whose veins, where flows no blood at all,
For ever the slow waters of green Lethe crawl.

E. ST. V. M.

SPLEEN [IV]

Quand le ciel bas et lourd pèse comme un couvercle
Sur l'esprit gémissant en proie aux longs ennuis,
Et que de l'horizon embrassant tout le cercle
Il nous verse un jour noir plus triste que les nuits;

Quand la terre est changée en un cachot humide,
Où l'Espérance, comme une chauve-souris,
S'en va battant les murs de son aile timide
Et se cognant la tête à des plafonds pourris;

Quand la pluie étalant ses immenses traînées
D'une vaste prison imite les barreaux,
Et qu'un peuple muet d'infâmes araignées
Vient tendre ses filets au fond de nos cerveaux,

Des cloches tout à coup sautent avec furie
Et lancent vers le ciel un affreux hurlement,
Ainsi que des esprits errants et sans patrie
Qui se mettent à geindre opiniâtrément.

WHEN THE LOW, HEAVY SKY

When the low, heavy sky weighs like the giant lid
Of a great pot upon the spirit crushed by care,
And from the whole horizon encircling us is shed
A day blacker than night, and thicker with despair;

When Earth becomes a dungeon, where the timid bat
Called Confidence, against the damp and slippery walls
Goes beating his blind wings, goes feebly bumping at
The rotted, mouldy ceiling, and the plaster falls;

When, dark and dropping straight, the long lines of the rain
Like prison-bars outside the window cage us in;
And silently, about the caught and helpless brain,
We feel the spider walk, and test the web, and spin;

Then all the bells at once ring out in furious clang,
Bombarding heaven with howling, horrible to hear,
Like lost and wandering souls, that whine in shrill **harangue**
Their obstinate complaints to an unlistening ear.

—*Et de longs corbillards, sans tambours ni musique,*
Défilent lentement dans mon âme; l'Espoir,
Vaincu, pleure, et l'Angoisse atroce, despotique,
Sur mon crâne incliné plante son drapeau noir.

—And a long line of hearses, with neither dirge nor drums,
Begins to cross my soul. Weeping, with steps that lag,
Hope walks in chains; and Anguish, after long wars, becomes
Tyrant at last, and plants on me his inky flag.

E. ST. V. M.

UN VOYAGE A CYTHÈRE

Mon cœur, comme un oiseau, voltigeait tout joyeux
Et planait librement à l'entour des cordages;
Le navire roulait sous un ciel sans nuages,
Comme un ange enivré du soleil radieux.

Quelle est cette île triste et noire?—C'est Cythère,
Nous dit-on, un pays fameux dans les chansons,
Eldorado banal de tous les vieux garçons.
Regardez, après tout, c'est une pauvre terre.

—Ile des doux secrets et des fêtes du cœur!
De l'antique Vénus le superbe fantôme
Au-dessus de tes mers plane comme un arome,
Et charge les esprits d'amour et de langueur.

Belle île aux myrtes verts, pleine de fleurs écloses,
Vénérée à jamais par toute nation,
Où les soupirs des cœurs en adoration
Roulent comme l'encens sur un jardin de roses

A VOYAGE TO CYTHERA

My heart, that seemed a bird, was flying in the sun
Before the mast—was flying joyously ahead:
The ship, too, like an angel, all her sails outspread,
Calmly beneath the unclouded sky flew on and on.

What is that sombre island? what dreary port of call?
"Cythera," someone laughs—"the legend of the seas,
Time-honoured Eldorado of aging debauchees.
Look! It is only a poor, bleak country, after all."

—O island of sweet revels and the sounding lyre!
O shore of unimaginable secrets, where
The shade of Venus walks upon the twilight air,
Drugging the very soul with languor and desire!

O island of green myrtles never withering!
Thy long renown, by every human tongue confessed,
To the far-scattered nations of the east and west
Is wafted, like the perfume of an endless spring

Ou le roucoulement éternel d'un ramier
—Cythère n'était plus qu'un terrain des plus maigres
Un désert rocailleux troublé par des cris aigres.
J'entrevoyais pourtant un objet singulier:

Ce n'était pas un temple aux ombres bocagères,
Où la jeune prêtresse, amoureuse des fleurs,
Allait, le corps brûlé de secrètes chaleurs,
Entre-bâillant sa robe aux brises passagères;

Mais voilà qu'en rasant la côte d'assez près
Pour troubler les oiseaux avec nos voiles blanches
Nous vîmes que c'était un gibet à trois branches,
Du ciel se détachant en noir, comme un cyprès.

De féroces oiseaux perchés sur leur pâture
Détruisaient avec rage un pendu déjà mûr,
Chacun plantant, comme un outil, son bec impur
Dans tous les coins saignants de cette pourriture;

Les yeux étaient deux trous, et du ventre effondré
Les intestins pesants lui coulaient sur les cuisses,
Et ses bourreaux gorgés de hideuses délices
L'avaient à coups de bec absolument châtré.

Or like a dove's nostalgic and eternal moan!
—Cythera had become, in truth, a wretched land,
A sullen desert glittering with rock and sand:
I saw along those shores one sign of life alone.

It was no antique temple nor the ruin thereof,
Where a young priestess wanders, her light robes unpent,
Confusing with the scent of flowers the virgin scent
Of her slim body secretly aflame for love.

No; but we could see clearly, having come so nigh
That the shore-birds were scolding and beating upon our sails,
A solitary gibbet constructed of three rails,
Funereal as a tall dead cypress against the sky.

Some vultures were destroying with energy and address
A hanged man, ripe already by perhaps a week—
Each planting carefully, like a sharp tool, his beak
In every corner of that dangling rottenness.

The eyes were holes; from the torn groin meandering
On to the thighs, streamed down the intestines blue and bright;
Not to be cheated of any possible delight,
Those birds had absolutely castrated the poor thing.

Sous les pieds, un troupeau de jaloux quadrupèdes,
Le museau relevé, tournoyait et rôdait;
Une plus grande bête au milieu s'agitait
Comme un exécuteur entourè de ses aides.

Habitant de Cythère, enfant d'un ciel si beau,
Silencieusement tu souffrais ces insultes
En expiation de tes infâmes cultes
Et des péchés qui t'ont interdit le tombeau.

Ridicule pendu, tes douleurs sont les miennes!
Je sentis à l'aspect de tes membres flottants,
Comme un vomissement, remonter vers mes dents
Le long fleuve de fiel des douleurs anciennes;

Devant toi, pauvre diable au souvenir si cher,
J'ai senti tous les becs et toutes les mâchoires
Des corbeaux lancinants et des panthères noires
Qui jadis aimaient tant à triturer ma chair.

—Le ciel était charmant, la mer était unie;
Pour moi tout était noir et sanglant désormais,
Hélas! et j'avais, comme en un suaire épais,
Le cœur enseveli dans cette allégorie.

Below, a pack of jealous wolves, impatient for
The still suspended, speedily diminishing feast,
Wove round with lifted muzzles. One gigantic beast
Was like an executioner among his corps.

Son of Cythera! remnant of a world so brave!
How silently, with thy black hollow eyes of woe,
Didst thou hang there, in payment for I do not know
What desperate crime forbidding thee an honest grave.

Helpless and abject creature! Who art thou but I?
Beholding thee, I could feel rise into my breast,
Like a long bitter vomit, all the sick repressed
Griefs and humiliations of the years gone by.

At sight of thee, poor devil, I could feel the whole
Rage of the past upon me—every beak and tooth
Of those wild birds and animals that in my youth
Loved tirelessly to lacerate my flesh and soul.

—The sea was calm and beautiful, the sky was clear:
What shadow covered them and hid them from my eyes?
The shadow cast by that symbolic tree! It lies
Upon my heart like a black pall for ever, I fear.

Dans ton île, ô Vénus! je n'ai trouvé debout
Qu'un gibet symbolique où pendait mon image.
—Ah! Seigneur! donnez-moi la force et le courage
De contempler mon cœur et mon corps sans dégoût!

Naught else, O Venus, in thy whole dominion—just
That mournful allegory to greet me, in my hour.
Almighty God! Give me the courage and the power
To contemplate my own true image without disgust!

G. D.

LE CRÉPUSCULE DU MATIN

La diane chantait dans les cours des casernes,
Et le vent du matin soufflait sur les lanternes.

C'était l'heure où l'essaim des rêves malfaisants
Tord sur leurs oreillers les bruns adolescents;
Où, comme un œil sanglant qui palpite et qui bouge,
La lampe sur le jour fait une tache rouge;
Où l'âme, sous le poids du corps revêche et lourd,
Imite les combats de la lampe et du jour.
Comme un visage en pleurs que les brises essuient,
L'air est plein du frisson des choses qui s'enfuient,
Et l'homme est las d'écrire et la femme d'aimer.

Les maisons çà et là commençaient à fumer.
Les femmes de plaisir, la paupière livide,
Bouche ouverte, dormaient de leur sommeil stupide;
Les pauvresses, traînant leurs seins maigres et froids,
Soufflaient sur leurs tisons et soufflaient sur leurs doigts.
C'était l'heure où parmi le froid et la lésine
S'aggravent les douleurs des femmes en gésine;

DAWN

Outside the barracks now the bugle called, and woke
The morning wind, which rose, making the lanterns smoke.

It was that hour when tortured dreams of stealthy joys
Twist in their beds the thin brown bodies of growing boys;
When, like a blood-shot eye that blinks and looks away,
The lamp still burns, and casts a red stain on the day;
When the soul, pinned beneath the body's weight and brawn,
Strives, as the lamplight strives to overcome the dawn;
The air, like a sad face whose tears the breezes dry,
Is tremulous with countless things about to die;
And men grow tired of writing, and women of making love.

Blue smoke was curling now from the cold chimneys of
A house or two; with heavy lids, mouths open wide,
Prostitutes slept their slumber dull and stupefied;
While labourers' wives got up, with sucked-out breasts, and stood
Blowing first on their hands, then on the flickering wood.
It was that hour when cold, and lack of things they need,
Combine, and women in childbirth have it hard indeed.

Comme un sanglot coupé par un sang écumeux
Le chant du coq au loin déchirait l'air brumeux,
Une mer de brouillards baignait les édifices,
Et les agonisants dans le fond des hospices
Poussaient leur dernier râle en hoquets inégaux.
Les débauchés rentraient, brisés par leurs travaux.

L'aurore grelottante en robe rose et verte
S'avançait lentement sur la Seine déserte,
Et le sombre Paris, en se frottant les yeux,
Empoignait ses outils—vieillard laborieux.

Like a sob choked by frothy hemorrhage, somewhere
Far-off a sudden cock-crow tore the misty air;
A sea of fog rolled in, effacing roofs and walls;
The dying, that all night in the bare hospitals
Had fought for life, grew weaker, rattled, and fell dead;
And gentlemen, debauched and drunk, swayed home to bed.

Aurora now in a thin dress of green and rose,
With chattering teeth advanced. Old sombre Paris rose,
Picked up its tools, and, over the deserted Seine,
Yawning, rubbing its eyes, slouched forth to work again.

E. ST. V. M.

LA MORT DES PAUVRES

C'est la Mort qui console, hélas! et qui fait vivre;
C'est le but de la vie, et c'est le seul espoir
Qui, comme un élixir, nous monte et nous enivre,
Et nous donne le cœur de marcher jusqu'au soir;

A travers la tempête, et la neige et le givre,
C'est la clarté vibrante à notre horizon noir;
C'est l'auberge fameuse inscrite sur le livre,
Où l'on pourra manger, et dormir, et s'asseoir;

C'est un Ange qui tient dans ses doigts magnétiques
Le sommeil et le don des rêves extatiques,
Et qui refait le lit des gens pauvres et nus;

C'est la gloire des Dieux, c'est le grenier mystique,
C'est la bourse du pauvre et sa patrie antique,
C'est le portique ouvert sur les Cieux inconnus!

THE DEATH OF THE POOR

Death? Death is our one comfort!—is the bread whereby
We live, the wine that warms us when all hope is gone;
The very goal of Life. That we shall one day die:
This is the thought which gives us courage to go on.

Clear on the black horizon, through the blinding sleet,
That beacon burns;—oh, Death, thou inn of wide renown!
Is it not written in the book: "Here all may eat;
Here there is rest for all; here all may sit them down"?

Thou hovering Angel, holding in thy magic hand
Slumber and blissful dreams; thou Glory overhead;
Mysterious attic, filled with treasures manifold;

The poor man's purse, and his remembered fatherland;
Thou, that remakest nightly the beggar's crumpled bed;
Thou only door ajar, pledge of the peace foretold!

E. ST. V. M.

PAYSAGE

Je veux, pour composer chastement mes églogues,
Coucher auprès du ciel, comme les astrologues,
Et, voisin des clochers, écouter en rêvant
Leurs hymnes solennels emportés par le vent.
Les deux mains au menton, du haut de ma mansarde,
Je verrai l'atelier qui chante et qui bavarde;
Les tuyaux, les clochers, ces mâts de la cité,
Et les grands ciels qui font rêver d'éternité.

Il est doux, à travers les brumes, de voir naître
L'étoile dans l'azur, la lampe à la fenêtre,
Les fleuves de charbon monter au firmament
Et la lune verser son pâle enchantement.
Je verrai les printemps, les étés, les automnes;
Et quand viendra l'hiver aux neiges monotones,
Je fermerai partout portières et volets
Pour bâtir dans la nuit mes féeriques palais.

Alors je rêverai des horizons bleuâtres,
Des jardins, des jets d'eau pleurant dans les albâtres,

LANDSCAPE

I want to write a book of chaste and simple verse,
Sleep in an attic, like the old astrologers,
Up near the sky, and hear upon the morning air
The tolling of the bells. I want to sit and stare,
My chin in my two hands, out on the humming shops,
The weathervanes, the chimneys, and the steepletops
That rise like masts above the city, straight and tall,
And the mysterious big heavens over all.

I want to watch the blue mist of the night come on,
The windows and the stars illumined, one by one,
The rivers of dark smoke pour upward lazily,
And the moon rise and turn them silver. I shall see
The springs, the summers, and the autumns slowly pass;
And when old Winter puts his blank face to the glass,
I shall close all my shutters, pull the curtains tight,
And build me stately palaces by candlelight.

And I shall dream of luxuries beyond surmise,
Gardens that are a stairway into azure skies,

Des baisers, des oiseaux chantant soir et matin,
Et tout ce que l'Idylle a de plus enfantin.
L'Émeute, tempêtant vainement à ma vitre,
Ne fera pas lever mon front de mon pupitre;
Car je serai plongé dans cette volupté
D'évoquer le Printemps avec ma volonté,
De tirer un soleil de mon cœur et de faire
De mes pensers brûlants une tiède atmosphère.

Fountains that weep in alabaster, birds that sing
All day—of every childish and idyllic thing.
'A revolution thundering in the street below
Will never lure me from my task, I shall be so
Lost in that quiet ecstasy, the keenest still,
Of calling back the springtime at my own free will,
Of feeling a sun rise within me, fierce and hot,
And make a whole bright landscape of my burning thought.

G. D.

LE SOLEIL

Le long du vieux faubourg, où pendent aux masures
Les persiennes, abri des secrètes luxures,
Quand le soleil cruel frappe à traits redoublés
Sur la ville et les champs, sur les toits et les blés,
Je vais m'exercer seul à ma fantasque escrime,
Flairant dans tous les coins les hasards de la rime,
Trébuchant sur les mots comme sur les pavés,
Heurtant parfois des vers depuis longtemps rêvés.

Ce père nourricier, ennemi des chloroses,
Éveille dans les champs les vers comme les roses;
Il fait s'évaporer les soucis vers le ciel,
Et remplit les cerveaux et les ruches de miel.
C'est lui qui rajeunit les porteurs de béquilles
Et les rend gais et doux comme des jeunes filles,
Et commande aux moissons de croître et de mûrir
Dans le cœur immortel qui toujours veut fleurir!

THE SUN

In this old district, where the shabby houses hide
Behind drawn shutters many a furtive lust inside,
In the fierce rays of noon, which mercilessly beat
On town and country, on the roofs and on the wheat,
I walk alone, absorbed in my fantastic play,—
Fencing with rhymes, which, parrying nimbly, back away;
Tripping on words, as on rough paving in the street,
Or bumping into verses I long had dreamed to meet.

The sun, our nourishing father, anaemia's deadly foe,
Makes poems, as if poems were roses, bud and grow;
Burns through the anxious mists of every mind alive,
And fills with honey the celled brain as the celled hive.
'Tis he who makes the man on crutches stump along
As gay as a young girl, humming as sweet a song;
Calls to the human spirit to climb and ripen still—
Which would bloom on for ever, could it have its will.

Quand, ainsi qu'un poète, il descend dans les villes.
Il ennoblit le sort des choses les plus viles,
Et s'introduit en roi, sans bruit et sans valets,
Dans tous les hôpitaux et dans tous les palais.

He goes into the city, where, like the poet, his light
Ennobles and gives purpose to the least thing in sight;
Or, quietly, unattended, like a king, he calls
At every palace, and visits all the hospitals.

E. ST. V. M.

LES SEPT VIEILLARDS

Fourmillante cité, cité pleine de rêves,
Où le spectre en plein jour raccroche le passant!
Les mystères partout coulent comme des sèves
Dans les canaux étroits du colosse puissant.

Un matin, cependant que dans la triste rue
Les maisons, dont la brume allongeait la hauteur,
Simulaient les deux quais d'une rivière accrue,
Et que, décor semblable à l'âme de l'acteur,

Un brouillard sale et jaune inondait tout l'espace,
Je suivais, roidissant mes nerfs comme un héros
Et discutant avec mon âme déjà lasse,
Le faubourg secoué par les lourds tombereaux.

Tout à coup, un vieillard dont les guenilles jaunes
Imitaient la couleur de ce ciel pluvieux,
Et dont l'aspect aurait fait pleuvoir les aumônes,
Sans la méchanceté qui luisait dans ses yeux,

THE SEVEN OLD MEN

City swarming with people, how full you are of dreams!
Here in broad daylight, surely, the passer-by may meet
A spectre,—be accosted by him! Mystery seems
To move like a thick sap through every narrow street.

I thought (daybreak, it was, in a sad part of town)
"These houses look much higher in the fog!"—they stood
Like two grey quays between which a muddy stream flows down;
The setting of the play matched well the actor's mood.

All space became a dirty yellow fog; I tried
To fight it off; I railed at my poor soul, whose feet,
Weary already, dragged and stumbled at my side.
Big wagons, bound for market, began to shake the street.

Suddenly there beside me an old man—all in holes
His garments were, and yellow, like the murky skies,
A sight to wring a rain of coins from kindly souls,
Save for a certain malice gleaming in his eyes,—

M'apparut. On eût dit sa prunelle trempée
Dans le fiel; son regard aiguisait les frimas,
Et sa barbe à longs poils, roide comme une épée,
Se projetait, pareille à celle de Judas.

Il n'était pas voûté, mais cassé, son échine
Faisant avec sa jambe un parfait angle droit,
Si bien que son bâton, parachevant sa mine,
Lui donnait la tournure et le pas maladroit

D'un quadrupède infirme ou d'un juif à trois pattes.
Dans la neige et la boue il allait s'empêtrant,
Comme s'il écrasait des morts sous ses savates,
Hostile à l'univers plutôt qu'indifférent.

Son pareil le suivait: barbe, œil, dos, bâton, loques,
Nul trait ne distinguait, du même enfer venu,
Ce jumeau centenaire, et ces spectres baroques
Marchaient du même pas vers un but inconnu.

A quel complot infâme étais-je donc en butte,
Ou quel méchant hasard ainsi m'humiliait?
Car je comptai sept fois, de minute en minute,
Ce sinistre vieillard qui se multipliait!

Appeared. You would have said those eyeballs, without doubt,
Were steeped in bile—they sharpened the sleet they looked upon.
His beard, with its long hairs, stiff as a sword stood out
Before him, as the beard of Judas must have done.

He stooped so when he walked, his spine seemed not so much
Bending as broken,—truly, his leg with his back-bone
Made a right angle; and his stick, the finishing touch,
Gave him the awkward gait—now rearing, now half-thrown—

Of a three-legged Jew, or some lame quadruped.
It crossed my mind, as through the mud and snow he went,
"He walks like someone crushing the faces of the dead.
Hostile, that's what he is; he's not indifferent."

A man exactly like him followed him. From beard
To stick they were the same, had risen from the same hell.
These centenarian twins kept step in rhythmic weird
Precision, toward some goal which doubtless they knew well.

"What ugly game is this?" I said; "what horseplay's here?
Am I the butt of knaves, or have I lost my mind?"
For seven times—I counted them—there did appear
This sinister form, which passed, yet left itself behind.

Que celui-là qui rit de mon inquiétude,
Et qui n'est pas saisi d'un frisson fraternel,
Songe bien que malgré tant de décrépitude
Ces sept monstres hideux avaient l'air éternel!

Aurais-je, sans mourir, contemplé le huitième,
Sosie inexorable, ironique et fatal,
Dégoûtant Phénix, fils et père de lui-même?
—Mais je tournai le dos au cortège infernal.

Exaspéré comme un ivrogne qui voit double,
Je rentrai, je fermai ma porte, épouvanté,
Malade et morfondu, l'esprit fiévreux et trouble,
Blessé par le mystère et par l'absurdité!

Vainement ma raison voulait prendre la barre;
La tempête en jouant déroutait ses efforts,
Et mon âme dansait, dansait, vieille gabarre
Sans mâts, sur une mer monstrueuse et sans bords!

Let anyone who smiles at my distress, whose heart
No sympathetic horror grips, consider well:
Though these old monsters seemed about to fall apart,
Somehow I knew they were eternal,—I could tell!

Had I beheld one more of them, I think indeed
I should have died!—for each, in some disgusting way,
Had spawned himself, lewd Phoenix, from his own foul seed,
Was his own son and father,—I fled—I could not stay.

Angry, bewildered, like a drunken man by whom
All objects are seen double, I locked my door, and heard
My frozen heart cry out with dread in the hot room,—
That what was so mysterious should be so absurd!

My reason fought to gain the bridge and take the helm;
The tempest thrust it back; and rudderless, unrigged,
A hull which the waves wash but will not overwhelm,
My soul upon a shoreless sea of horror jigged.

E. ST. V. M.

LE VIN DE L'ASSASSIN

Ma femme est morte, je suis libre!
Je puis donc boire tout mon soûl.
Lorsque je rentrais sans un sou,
Ses cris me déchiraient la fibre.

Autant qu'un roi je suis heureux;
L'air est pur, le ciel admirable . . .
—Nous avions un été semblable
Lorsque je devins amoureux!

—L'horrible soif qui me déchire
Aurait besoin pour s'assouvir
D'autant de vin qu'en peut tenir
Son tombeau;—ce n'est pas peu dire:

Je l'ai jetée au fond d'un puits,
Et j'ai même poussé sur elle
Tous les pavés de la margelle.
—Je l'oublierai si je le puis!

THE DRUNKARD

My wife is dead, and I am free!
Now I can drink both night and day.
When I came home without my pay
Her crying upset me horribly.

I am as happy as a king.
The air is soft. The sky is clear.
Ah, what a lovely spring, this year!
I courted her in such a spring.

Now I can drink to drown my care
As much wine as her tomb would hold—
The tomb where she lies pale and cold.
And that will be no small affair,

For I have thrown her, body and limb,
In an old well; I even threw
All the loose stones around the brim
On top of her. Good riddance, too!

Au nom des serments de tendresse,
Dont rien ne peut nous délier,
Et pour nous réconcilier
Comme au beau temps de notre ivresse,

J'implorai d'elle un rendez-vous,
Le soir, sur une route obscure,
Elle y vint! folle créature!
—Nous sommes tous plus ou moins fous!

Elle était encore jolie,
Quoique bien fatiguée! et moi,
Je l'aimai trop;—voilà pourquoi
Je lui dis: Sors de cette vie!

Nul ne peut me comprendre. Un seul
Parmi ces ivrognes stupides
Songea-t-il dans ses nuits morbides
A faire du vin un linceul?

Cette crapule invulnérable
Comme les machines de fer
Jamais, ni l'été ni l'hiver,
N'a connu l'amour véritable,

I asked her in the name of Christ,
To whom our marriage vows were told,
To be my sweetheart as of old—
To come to a forsaken tryst

We had when we were young and gay,
That everything might be the same:
And she, the foolish creature, came!
We all have our weak moments, eh?

She was attractive still, all right,
Though faded. I still loved her—more
Than there was rhyme or reason for.
I had to end it, come what might!

Nobody understands me. What's
The use of wasting my good breath
Explaining to these stupid sots
The mysteries of love and death?

They take their women by routine,
These louts—the way they eat and drink.
Which one has ever stopped to think
What the word love might really mean?

Avec ses noirs enchantements,
Son cortège infernal d'alarmes,
Ses fioles de poison, ses larmes,
Ses bruits de chaîne et d'ossements!

—Me voilà libre et solitaire!
Je serai ce soir ivre-mort;
Alors, sans peur et sans remord,
Je me coucherai sur la terre,

Et je dormirai comme un chien.
Le chariot aux lourdes roues
Chargé de pierres et de boues,
Le wagon enrayé peut bien

Écraser ma tête coupable,
Ou me couper par le milieu,
Je m'en moque comme de Dieu,
Du Diable ou de la Sainte Table!

Love, with its softness in your reins,
With all its nightmares, all its fears,
Its cups of poison mixed with tears,
Its rattling skeletons and chains.

—Well, here I am, alone and free!
Tonight I will be drunk for' fair,
And I will lay me down, I swear,
Upon the highroad happily,

And sleep like an old dog, be sure,
Right where the heavy trucks go by,
Loaded with gravel and manure.
The wheel can smear my brains out—ay,

Or it can break me like a clod
In two, or it can mash me flat.
I care about as much for that
As for the long white beard of God!

G. D.

BRUMES ET PLUIES

O fins d'automne, hivers, printemps trempés de boue,
Endormeuses saisons! je vous aime et vous loue
D'envelopper ainsi mon cœur et mon cerveau
D'un linceul vaporeux et d'un vague tombeau.

Dans cette grande plaine où l'autan froid se joue,
Où par les longues nuits la girouette s'enroue,
Mon âme mieux qu'au temps du tiède renouveau
Ouvrira largement ses ailes de corbeau.

Rien n'est plus doux au cœur plein de choses funèbres,
Et sur qui dès longtemps descendent les frimas,
O blafardes saisons, reines de nos climats!

Que l'aspect permanent de vos pâles ténèbres,
—Si ce n'est par un soir sans lune, deux à deux,
D'endormir la douleur sur un lit hasardeux.

MISTS AND RAINS

O ends of autumn, winters, springtimes deep in mud,
Seasons of drowsiness,—my love and gratitude
I give you, that have wrapped with mist my heart and brain
As with a shroud, and shut them in a tomb of rain.

In this wide land when coldly blows the bleak south-west
And weather-vanes at night grow hoarse on the house-crest,
Better than in the time when green things bud and grow
My mounting soul spreads wide its black wings of a crow.

The heart filled up with gloom, and to the falling sleet
Long since accustomed, finds no other thing more sweet—
O dismal seasons, queens of our sad climate crowned—

Than to remain always in your pale shadows drowned;
(Unless it be, some dark night, kissing an unseen head,
To rock one's pain to sleep upon a hazardous bed.)

E. ST. V. M.

CORRESPONDANCES

La Nature est un temple où de vivants piliers
Laissent parfois sortir de confuses paroles;
L'homme y passe à travers des forêts de symboles
Qui l'observent avec des regards familiers.

Comme de longs échos qui de loin se confondent
Dans une ténébreuse et profonde unité,
Vaste comme la nuit et comme la clarté,
Les parfums, les couleurs et les sons se répondent.

Il est des parfums frais comme des chairs d'enfants,
Doux comme les hautbois, verts comme les prairies,
—Et d'autres, corrompus, riches et triomphants,

Ayant l'expansion des choses infinies,
Comme l'ambre, le musc, le benjoin et l'encens,
Qui chantent les transports de l'esprit et des sens.

CORRESPONDENCES

All nature is one temple, the living aisles whereof
Murmur in a soft language, half strange, half understood;
Man wanders there as through a cabalistic wood,
Aware of eyes that watch him in the leaves above.

Like voices echoing in his senses from beyond
Life's watery source, and which into one voice unite,
Vast as the turning planet clothed in darkness and light,
So do all sounds and hues and fragrances correspond.

Perfumes there are as sweet as the music of pipes and strings,
As pure as the naked flesh of children, as full of peace
As wide green prairies—and there are others, having the whole

Corrupt proud all-pervasiveness of infinite things,
Like frankincense, and musk, and myrrh, and ambergris,
That cry of the ecstasy of the body and of the soul.

G. D.

DON JUAN AUX ENFERS

Quand don Juan descendit vers l'onde souterraine,
Et lorsqu'il eut donné son obole à Charon,
Un sombre mendiant, l'œil fier comme Antisthène,
D'un bras vengeur et fort saisit chaque aviron.

Montrant leurs seins pendants et leurs robes ouvertes,
Des femmes se tordaient sous le noir firmament,
Et, comme un grand troupeau de victimes offertes,
Derrière lui traînaient un long mugissement.

Sganarelle en riant lui réclamait ses gages,
Tandis que don Luis avec un doigt tremblant
Montrait à tous les morts errant sur les rivages
Le fils audacieux qui railla son front blanc.

Frissonnant sous son deuil, la chaste et maigre Elvire,
Près de l'époux perfide et qui fut son amant
Semblait lui réclamer un suprême sourire
Où brillât la douceur de son premier serment.

DON JUAN IN HADES

He found the wide bark rocking in the Stygian breeze
And came aboard, having first paid Charon what he owed.
A beggar, sombre and haughty as Antisthenes,
Seized the long oars with a revengeful gesture and rowed.

Writhing and tearing open their garments while he crossed,
A crowd of disappointed females, herded there
Along the bank like victims for a holocaust,
Filled with a soft and bestial moaning the dark air.

Sganarelle laughed triumphantly, demanding his wage;
Don Luis, still wrathful, pointed with a palsied hand
To the unruly son who mocked him in his old age,
Calling to witness the dead throngs upon that strand.

She whom he wed in church and loved a little while,
Elvira, thin and trembling in her black robes of grief,
Seemed to implore of her betrayer a last smile
In memory of his first ardour, noble and brief.

Tout droit dans son armure, un grand homme de pierre
Se tenait à la barre et coupait le flot noir;
Mais le calme héros, courbé sur sa rapière,
Regardait le sillage et ne daignait rien voir.

The knight he murdered and whose ghost he had rebuked
Stood now, a tall and cuirassed helmsman, at the stem;
But the calm hero, leaning upon his rapier, looked
Absently into the water, ignoring all of them.

G. D.

UNE MARTYRE

Au milieu des flacons, des étoffes lamées
Et des meubles voluptueux,
Des marbres, des tableaux, des robes parfumées
Qui traînent à plis somptueux,

Dans une chambre tiède où, comme en une serre,
L'air est dangereux et fatal,
Où des bouquets mourants dans leurs cercueils de verre
Exhalent leur soupir final,

Un cadavre sans tête épanche, comme un fleuve,
Sur l'oreiller désaltéré
Un sang rouge et vivant, dont la toile s'abreuve
Avec l'avidité d'un pré.

Semblable aux visions pâles qu'enfante l'ombre
Et qui nous enchaînent les yeux,
La tête, avec l'amas de sa crinière sombre
Et de ses bijoux précieux,

MURDERED WOMAN

DRAWING OF AN UNKNOWN MASTER

Flasks of expensive scent, embroideries, rich brocades,
    Taffeta sofas, satin chairs;
Statues in marble, paintings; fragrance that pervades
    The empty, sumptuous gowns; warm airs

And sweet,—yet sultry, damp, unhealthful to inhale:
    That sickening green-house atmosphere
Dying bouquets in their glass coffins give—a stale
    Voluptuous chamber. . . . Lying here

A corpse without a head, whence flows in a bright stream,
    Making an ever broadening stain,
The red and living blood, which the white pillows seem
    To lap up like a thirsty plain.

Pale as those awful shapes that out of shadow stare,
    Chaining our helpless eyes to theirs,
The head, with its great mass of rich and sombre hair—
    The ear-rings still in the small ears—

Sur la table de nuit, comme une renoncule,
  Repose, et, vide de pensers,
Un regard vague et blanc comme le crépuscule
  S'échappe des yeux révulsés.

Sur le lit, le tronc nu sans scrupules étale
  Dans le plus complet abandon
La secrète splendeur et la beauté fatale
  Dont la nature lui fit don;

Un bas rosâtre, orné de coins d'or, à la jambe
  Comme un souvenir est resté;
La jarretière, ainsi qu'un œil secret qui flambe,
  Darde un regard diamanté.

Le singulier aspect de cette solitude
  Et d'un grand portrait langoureux,
Aux yeux provocateurs comme son attitude,
  Révèle un amour ténébreux,

Une coupable joie et des fêtes étranges
  Pleines de baisers infernaux,
Dont se réjouissait l'essaim de mauvais anges
  Nageant dans les plis des rideaux;

Et cependant, à voir la maigreur élégante
  De l'épaule au contour heurté,
La hanche un peu pointue et la taille fringante
  Ainsi qu'un reptile irrité,

[204]

Like a ranunculus on the night-table sits;
    And, void of thought, blank as the light
Of dawn, a glinting vague regard escapes from its
    Eyeballs, up-rolled and china-white.

The headless trunk, in shameless posture on the bed,
    Naked, in loose abandon lies,
Its secret parts exposed, its treasures all outspread
    As if to charm a lover's eyes.

One sequined stocking, pink against the milky thigh,
    Remains, pathetic souvenir;
The jeweled garter, like a flashing, secret eye,
    Darts and withdraws a diamond leer.

A languorous portrait on the wall contrives to give
    Force to the singular effect
Of the deep solitude,—the eyes provocative,
    The pose inviting, half-erect.

The ghost of something strange and guilty, of some feast
    Involving most improper fare,
Demoniac kisses, all obscure desires released,
    Swims in the silent curtains there.

And yet, that fragile shoulder, that fine hand and arm—
    How delicate the curve they make!—
The pelvic bones so sweetly pointed, the whole form
    Lithe as a teased and fighting snake!—

Elle est bien jeune encor!—Son âme exaspérée
　　Et ses sens par l'ennui mordus
S'étaient-ils entr'ouverts à la meute altérée
　　Des désirs errants et perdus?

L'homme vindicatif que tu n'as pu, vivante,
　　Malgré tant d'amour, assouvir,
Combla-t-il sur ta chair inerte et complaisante
　　L' immensité de son désir?

Réponds, cadavre impur! et par tes tresses roides
　　Te soulevant d'un bras fiévreux,
Dis-moi, tête effrayante, a-t-il sur tes dents froides,
　　Collé les suprêmes adieux?

—Loin du monde railleur, loin de la foule impure,
　　Loin des magistrats curieux,
Dors en paix, dors en paix, étrange créature,
　　Dans ton tombeau mystérieux;

Ton époux court le monde, et ta forme immortelle
　　Veille près de lui quand il dort;
Autant que toi sans doute il te sera fidèle,
　　Et constant jusques à la mort.

She must have been quite young . . . her senses, all her soul,
    Avid for life and driven wild
By tedium, set ajar, it may be, to the whole
    Pack of perversions . . . ah, poor child!

Did he at length, that man, his awful thirst too great
    For living flesh to satisfy,
On this inert, obedient body consummate
    His lust?—O ravished corpse, reply!

Answer me, impure thing! Speak, frightening head, and tell:
    Lifting you up by your long hair,
Did he on your cold teeth imprint in last farewell
    One kiss, before he set you there?

Far from the mocking world, the peering crowd, oh far
    From inquest, coroner, magistrate,
Sleep; sleep in peace; I leave you lying as you are,
    Mysterious unfortunate.

In vain your lover roves the world; the thought of you
    Troubles each chamber where he lies:
Even as you are true to him, he will be true
    To you, no doubt, until he dies.

                        E. ST. V. M.

LE SQUELETTE LABOUREUR

I

Dans les planches d'anatomie
Qui traînent sur ces quais poudreux
Où maint livre cadavéreux
Dort comme une antique momie,

Dessins auxquels la gravité
Et le savoir d'un vieil artiste,
Bien que le sujet en soit triste,
Ont communiqué la Beauté,

On voit, ce qui rend plus complètes
Ces mystérieuses horreurs,
Bêchant comme des laboureurs,
Des Écorchés et des Squelettes.

SKELETONS DIGGING

I

Among the anatomical plates
Displayed along the dusty quays,
Where many a dead book desiccates
Like an old mummy—among these

Sad diagrams to which the grave
Fantasy and ironic skill
Of some forgotten artist have
Lent a mysterious beauty still,

One sees (for thus mere nerves and bones
Were rendered life-like through his pains)
Digging like labourers, skeletons
And skinless men composed of veins.

De ce terrain que vous fouillez.
Manants résignés et funèbres,
De tout l'effort de vos vertèbres,
Ou de vos muscles dépouillés,

Dites, quelle moisson étrange,
Forçats arrachés au charnier,
Tirez-vous, et de quel fermier
Avez-vous à remplir la grange?

Voulez-vous (d'un destin trop dur
Épouvantable et clair emblème!)
Montrer que dans la fosse même
Le sommeil promis n'est pas sûr;

Qu'envers nous le Néant est traître:
Que tout, même la Mort, nous ment,
Et que sempiternellement,
Hélas! il nous faudra peut-être

II

Out of that stony soil which ye
Unceasingly upturn, with all
The strength of your stripped vertebrae
And fleshless thews—funereal

Prisoners from the charnel pile!—
What do ye look for? Speak. What strange
Harvest prepare ye all this while?
What lord has bid you load his grange?

Do ye desire, O symbols clear
And frightful of a doom unguessed,
To demonstrate that even there,
In the deep grave, we have no rest—

That we can no more count as friend
Eternity than we can Time,
Death, too, being faithless in the end?
That we shall toil in dust and grime

Dans quelque pays inconnu
Écorcher la terre revêche
Et pousser une lourde bêche
Sous notre pied sanglant et nu?

For ever upon some field of shade,
And harry the stiff sod, and put
Over and over to the spade
A naked and ensanguined foot?

G. D.

JE N'AI PAS OUBLIÉ

Je n'ai pas oublié, voisine de la ville,
Notre blanche maison, petite mais tranquille,
Sa Pomone de plâtre et sa vieille Vénus
Dans un bosquet chétif cachant leurs membres nus;
Et le soleil, le soir, ruisselant et superbe,
Qui, derrière la vitre où se brisait sa gerbe,
Semblait, grand œil ouvert dans le ciel curieux,
Contempler nos dîners longs et silencieux,
Répandant largement ses beaux reflets de cierge
Sur la nappe frugale et les rideaux de serge.

A MEMORY

All this was long ago, but I do not forget
Our small white house, between the city and the farms;
The Venus, the Pomona,—I remember yet
How in the leaves they hid their chipping plaster charms;
And the majestic sun at evening, setting late,
Behind the pane that broke and scattered his bright rays,
How like an open eye he seemed to contemplate
Our long and silent dinners with a curious gaze:
The while his golden beams, like tapers burning there,
Made splendid the serge curtains and the simple fare.

E. ST. V. M.

LE BALCON

Mère des souvenirs, maîtresse des maîtresses,
O toi, tous mes plaisirs, ô toi, tous mes devoirs!
Tu te rappelleras la beauté des caresses,
La douceur du foyer et le charme des soirs,
Mère des souvenirs, maîtresse des maîtresses!

Les soirs illuminés par l'ardeur du charbon,
Et les soirs au balcon, voilés de vapeurs roses;
Que ton sein m'était doux! que ton cœur m'était bon!
Nous avons dit souvent d'impérissables choses
Les soirs illuminés par l'ardeur du charbon.

Que les soleils sont beaux dans les chaudes soirées!
Que l'espace est profond! que le cœur est puissant!
En me penchant vers toi, reine des adorées,
Je croyais respirer le parfum de ton sang.
Que les soleils sont beaux dans les chaudes soirées!

THE BALCONY

Inspirer of my youth, mistress beyond compare,
You who were all my pleasures, all my hopes and dreams!
Do you recall our cheerful room—our evenings there,
Quiet and passionate? Like yesterday, it seems,
Inspirer of my youth, mistress beyond compare!

The evenings lighted by the hushed flame of the coal,
The warm rose-misted twilights in the early springs,
The balcony! How I adored you, body and soul!
And, darling, we have said imperishable things
The evenings lighted by the hushed flame of the coal.

How splendid were the long slow summer sunsets, too!
How large the world appeared to us! How strong and good
Life ran then in our veins! When I leaned close to you
I thought that I could breathe the perfume of your blood.
How splendid were the long slow summer sunsets, too!

La nuit s'épaississait ainsi qu'une cloison,
Et mes yeux dans le noir devinaient tes prunelles
Et je buvais ton souffle, ô douceur, ô poison!
Et tes pieds s'endormaient dans mes mains fraternelles
La nuit s'épaississait ainsi qu'une cloison.

Je sais l'art d'évoquer les minutes heureuses,
Et revis mon passé blotti dans tes genoux.
Car à quoi bon chercher tes beautés langoureuses
Ailleurs qu'en ton cher corps et qu'en ton cœur si doux?
Je sais l'art d'évoquer les minutes heureuses!

Ces serments, ces parfums, ces baisers infinis,
Renaîtront-ils d'un gouffre interdit à nos sondes,
Comme montent au ciel les soleils rajeunis
Après s'être lavés au fond des mers profondes?
—O serments! ô parfums! ô baisers infinis!

The night would close around us like a dim blue wall,
And your eyes flashed within the darkness, and the sweet
Drug of your breath came over me. Do you recall
How I would love to lie for hours holding your feet?
The night would close around us like a dim blue wall.

I can relive the ecstasy that Time has slain;
At moments I can feel myself between your thighs.
What use to hope for anything like that again
With someone else? What use to seek in any wise?
I can relive the ecstasy that Time has slain.

Those cries, those long embraces, that remembered scent:
Can they be lost for ever? Will they not come round
Like stars, like suns, to blaze upon the firmament
Of future worlds, from the abyss we cannot sound?
—O cries! O long embraces! O remembered scent!

G. D.

LA PRIÈRE D'UN PAIEN

Ah! ne ralentis pas tes flammes;
Réchauffe mon cœur engourdi,
Volupté, torture des âmes!
Diva! supplicem exaudi!

Déesse dans l'air répandue,
Flamme dans notre souterrain!
Exauce une âme morfondue,
Qui te consacre un chant d'airain.

Volupté, sois toujours ma reine!
Prends le masque d'une sirène
Faite de chair et de velours,

Ou verse-moi tes sommeils lourds
Dans le vin informe et mystique,
Volupté, fantôme élastique!

THE PAGAN'S PRAYER

Ah, damp not yet the living coals!
Heat once again my heart in thee!
Voluptuousness, thou scourge of souls,
Goddess, incline thine ear to me!

Spirit abroad in the bright air,
Flame in our dark and secret ways,
Freezing I bring thee—grant my prayer!—
A song of brass to bruit thy praise!

Siren, be still my sovereign; keep
Thy kingdom; wear thy mask, whose mesh
Is half of velvet, half of flesh!

Or pour me out thy heavy sleep,
In mystic and amorphous wine:
Phantom elastic and divine.

E. ST. V. M.

RÉVERSIBILITÉ

Ange plein de gaîté, connaissez-vous l'angoisse,
La honte, les remords, les sanglots, les ennuis
Et les vagues terreurs de ces affreuses nuits
Qui compriment le cœur comme un papier qu'on froisse?
Ange plein de gaîté, connaissez-vous l'angoisse?

Ange plein de bonté, connaissez-vous la haine,
Les poings crispés dans l'ombre et des larmes de fiel,
Quand la Vengeance bat son infernal rappel,
Et de nos facultés se fait le capitaine?
Ange plein de bonté, connaissez-vous la haine?

Ange plein de santé, connaissez-vous les Fièvres,
Qui, le long des grands murs de l'hospice blafard,
Comme des exilés, s'en vont d'un pied traînard,
Cherchant le soleil rare et remuant les lèvres?
Ange plein de santé, connaissez-vous les Fièvres?

THE ANGELIC ONE

Spirit of happiness, hast thou heard tell of woe?
Hast thou heard tell of anguish, and remorse, and care—
Of those long nights when in the black fist of Despair
The heart is crumpled up like paper? Dost thou know,
Spirit of happiness? Hast thou heard tell of woe?

Spirit of kindliness, hast thou heard tell of hate,
The clenched hands in the darkness, the silent bitter tears,
With Vengeance beating in the arteries of our ears
Its dogged tom-tom, irresistible as fate?
Spirit of kindliness, hast thou heard tell of hate?

Spirit of health, hast thou heard whisper of Disease,
Whose pallid children, in the courtyard grey with soot
Of the bleak hospital, go dragging a slow foot
To find a patch of sunlight? Hast thou heard of these?
Spirit of health, hast thou heard whisper of Disease?

Ange plein de beauté, connaissez-vous les rides,
Et la peur de vieillir, et ce hideux tourment
De lire la secrète horreur du dévoûment
Dans des yeux où longtemps burent nos yeux avides?
Ange plein de beauté, connaissez-vous les rides?

Ange plein de bonheur, de joie et de lumières,
David mourant aurait demandé la santé
Aux émanations de ton corps enchanté!
Mais de toi je n'implore, ange, que tes prières,
Ange plein de bonheur, de joie et de lumières?

Spirit of beauty, hast thou heard of ugliness,
Of the long secret torment of growing old—above
All else, the pain of reading in the eyes we love
A wordless horror, even while the lips say "yes"?
Spirit of beauty, hast thou heard of ugliness?

Spirit of joy, spirit of beauty, spirit of light,
David, grown old, would have thought nothing to implore
Thy healing touch, thy warm young presence in the night;
But, spirit, I only ask of thee thy prayers, no more—
Spirit of joy, spirit of beauty, spirit of light!

G. D.

ÉLÉVATION

Au-dessus des étangs, au-dessus des vallées,
Des montagnes, des bois, des nuages, des mers,
Par delà le soleil, par delà les éthers,
Par delà les confins des spheres étoilées,

Mon esprit, tu te meus avec agilité,
Et, comme un bon nageur qui se pâme dans l'onde,
Tu sillonnes gaîment l'immensité profonde
Avec une indicible et mâle volupté.

Envole-toi bien loin de ces miasmes morbides,
Va te purifier dans l'air supérieur,
Et bois, comme une pure et divine liqueur,
Le feu clair qui remplit les espaces limpides.

Derrière les ennuis et les vastes chagrins
Qui chargent de leur poids l'existence brumeuse,
Heureux celui qui peut d'une aile vigoureuse
S'élancer vers les champs lumineux et sereins!

UP

Above the valleys, above the mountains, above the sea,
Above the mists that rise at morning from river and pond—
Beyond the sun, beyond the fringe of the ether, beyond
The boundaries of the fields of stars and nebulae,

With what deep bliss, with what insatiable delight,
My soul, like a good swimmer revelling in the wave,
You plunge into immensity! With what a grave
Mute joy you saturate yourself in the clear height!

Fly! Oh, indeed, fly far from this unwholesome place!
Go and be purged in radiance, wheeling higher and higher:
Be drunken, be washed through with the transparent fire,
Be lost in the serene bright solitudes of space!

From these low vapours hanging in the windless air,
From these miasmas fraught with ancient woe and ill,
Most blest, most fortunate is he who can at will
Take flight into a region luminous and fair—

Celui dont les pensers, comme des alouettes,
Vers les cieux le matin prennent un libre essor,
—Qui plane sur la vie et comprend sans effort
Le langage des fleurs et des choses muettes!

He whose unwearied thoughts on effortless light wings
Go up like larks at morning, and circle without fear
Above the wakening land—aloof and free—and hear
The voices of the flowers and of all voiceless things!

G. D.

LE VOYAGE

I

Pour l'enfant, amoureux de cartes et d'estampes,
L'univers est égal à son vaste appétit.
Ah! que le monde est grand à la clarté des lampes!
Aux yeux du souvenir que le monde est petit!

Un matin nous partons, le cerveau plein de flamme,
Le cœur gros de rancune et de désirs amers,
Et nous allons, suivant le rythme de la lame,
Berçant notre infini sur le fini des mers:

Les uns, joyeaux de fuir une patrie infâme;
D'autres, l'horreur de leurs berceaux, et quelques-uns,
Astrologues noyés dans les yeux d'une femme,
La Circé tyrannique aux dangereux parfums.

Pour n'être pas changés en bêtes, ils s'enivrent
D'espace et de lumière et de cieux embrasés;
La glace qui les mord, les soleils qui les cuivrent,
Effacent lentement la marque des baisers.

TRAVEL

I

The child, in love with globes and maps of foreign parts,
Finds in the universe no dearth and no defect.
How big the world is, seen by lamplight on his charts!
How very small the world is, viewed in retrospect.

Some morning we start out; we have a grudge, we itch
To hurt someone, get even,—whatever the cause may be,
Here we are, leaning to the vessel's roll and pitch,
Cradling our infinite upon the finite sea:

People who think their country shameful, who despise
Its politics, are here; and men who hate their home;
Astrologers, who read the stars in women's eyes
Till nearly drowned, stand by the rail and watch the foam;

Men who must run from Circe, or be changed to swine,
Go tramping round the deck, drunken with light and air,
Thinking that wind and sun and spray that tastes of brine
Can clean the lips of kisses, blow perfume from the hair.

Mais les vrais voyageurs sont ceux-là seuls qui partent
Pour partir; cœurs légers, semblables aux ballons,
De leur fatalité jamais ils ne s'écartent,
Et, sans savoir pourquoi, disent toujours: Allons!

Ceux-là dont les désirs ont la forme des nues,
Et qui rêvent, ainsi qu'un conscrit le canon,
De vastes voluptés, changeantes, inconnues,
Et dont l'esprit humain n'a jamais su le nom!

II

Nous imitons, horreur! la toupie et la boule
Dans leur valse et leurs bonds; même dans nos sommeils
La Curiosité nous tourmente et nous roule,
Comme un Ange cruel qui fouette des soleils.

Singulière fortune où le but se déplace,
Et, n'étant nulle part, peut être n'importe où!
Où l'Homme, dont jamais l'espérance n'est lasse,
Pour trouver le repos court toujours comme un fou!

Notre âme est un trois-mâts cherchant son Icarie;
Une voix retentit sur le pont: "Ouvre l'œil!"
Une voix de la hune, ardente et folle, crie:
"Amour . . . gloire . . . bonheur!" Enfer! c'est un écueil!

But the true travellers are those who leave a port
Just to be leaving; hearts light as balloons, they cry,
"Come on! There's a ship sailing! Hurry! Time's getting short!"
And pack a bag and board her,—and could not tell you why.

Those whose desires assume the shape of mist or cloud;
Who long for, as the raw recruit longs for his gun,
Voluptuousness immense and changing, by the crowd
Unguessed, and never known by name to anyone.

II

So, like a top, spinning and waltzing horribly,
Or bouncing like a ball, we go,—even in profound
Slumber tormented, rolled by Curiosity
Like hoops, as some hard Angel whips the suns around.

Bizarre phenomenon, this goal that changes place!—
And, being nowhere, can be any port of call!
Where Man, whose hope is never out of breath, will race
Madly, to find repose, just anywhere at all!

Our soul before the wind sails on, Utopia-bound;
A voice calls from the deck, "What's that ahead there?—land?"
A voice from the dark crow's-nest—wild, fanatic sound—
Shouts "Happiness! Glory! Love!"—it's just a bank of sand!

Chaque îlot signalé par l'homme de vigie
Est un Eldorado promis par le Destin;
L'Imagination qui dresse son orgie
Ne trouve qu'un récif aux clartés du matin.

O le pauvre amoureux des pays chimériques!
Faut-il le mettre aux fers, le jeter à la mer,
Ce matelot ivrogne, inventeur d'Amériques
Dont le mirage rend le gouffre plus amer?

Tel le vieux vagabond, piétinant dans la boue,
Rêve, le nez en l'air, de brillants paradis;
Son œil ensorcelé découvre une Capoue
Partout où la chandelle illumine un taudis.

III

Étonnants voyageurs! quelles nobles histoires
Nous lisons dans vos yeux profonds comme les mers!
Montrez-nous les écrins de vos riches mémoires,
Les bijoux merveilleux, faits d'astres et d'éthers.

Nous voulons voyager sans vapeur et sans voile!
Faites, pour égayer l'ennui de nos prisons,
Passer sur nos esprits, tendus comme une toile,
Vos souvenirs avec leurs cadres d'horizons.

Each little island sighted by the watch at night
Becomes an Eldorado, is in his belief
The Promised Land; Imagination soars; despite
The fact that every dawn reveals a barren reef.

Poor fellow, sick with love for that which never was!
Put him in irons—must we?—throw him overboard?
Mad, drunken tar, inventor of Americas . . .
Which, fading, make the void more bitter, more abhorred.

So the old trudging tramp, befouled by muck and mud,
Ever before his eyes keeps Paradise in sight,
And sniffs with nose in air a steaming Lotus-bud,
Wherever humble people sup by candlelight.

III

Astonishing, you are, you travellers,—your eyes
Are deep as the sea's self; what stories they withhold!
Open for us the chest of your rich memories!
Show us those treasures, wrought of meteoric gold!

We'd like, though not by steam or sail, to travel, too!
Brighten our prisons, please! Our days are all the same!
Paint on our spirits, stretched like canvases for you,
Your memories, that have horizons for their frame!

Dites, qu'avez-vous vu?

IV

"*Nous avons vu des astres*
Et des flots; nous avons vu des sables aussi;
Et, malgré bien des chocs et d'imprévus désastres,
Nous nous sommes souvent ennuyés, comme ici.

La gloire du soleil sur la mer violette,
La gloire des cités dans le soleil couchant,
Allumaient dans nos cœurs une ardeur inquiète
De plonger dans un ciel au reflet alléchant.

Les plus riches cités, les plus grands paysages,
Jamais ne contenaient l'attrait mystérieux
De ceux que le hasard fait avec les nuages,
Et toujours le désir nous rendait soucieux!

—*La jouissance ajoute au désir de la force.*
Désir, vieil arbre à qui le plaisir sert d'engrais,
Cependant que grossit et durcit ton écorce,
Tes branches veulent voir le soleil de plus près!

Tell us, what have you seen?

IV

"What have we seen?—oh, well,
We have seen waves, seen stars, seen quite a bit of sand;
We have been shipwrecked once or twice; but, truth to tell,
It's just as dull as here in any foreign land.

The glory of the sun upon the violet sea,
The glory of the castles in the setting sun,
Saddened us, made us restless, made us long to be
Under some magic sky, some unfamiliar one.

Truly, the finest cities, the most famous views,
Were never so attractive or mysterious
As those we saw in clouds. But it was all no use,
We had to keep on going—that's the way with us.

—Fulfillment only adds fresh fuel to the blaze.
(Desire!—old tree that pasture on pleasure and grow fat,
Your bark grows harder, thicker, with the passing days,
But you are set to reach the sun, for all of that!

Grandiras-tu toujours, grand arbre plus vivace
Que le cyprès?—Pourtant nous avons, avec soin
Cueilli quelques croquis pour votre album vorace,
Frères qui trouvez beau tout ce qui vient de loin!

Nous avons salué des idoles à trompe;
Des trônes constellés de joyaux lumineux;
Des palais ouvragés dont la féerique pompe
Serait pour vos banquiers un rêve ruineux;

Des costumes qui sont pour les yeux une ivresse;
Des femmes dont les dents et les ongles sont teints
Et des jongleurs savants que le serpent caresse."

V

Et puis, et puis encore?

VI

"O cerveaux enfantins!

Pour ne pas oublier la chose capitale,
Nous avons vu partout, et sans l'avoir cherché,
Du haut jusques en bas de l'échelle fatale,
Le spectacle ennuyeux de l'immortel péché:

Shall you grow on for ever, tall tree,—must you outdo
The cypress?) Still, we have collected, we may say,
For your voracious album, with care, a sketch or two,
Brothers, to whom all's fine that comes from far away.

We have bowed down to bestial idols; we have seen
Baldaquined thrones inlaid with every kind of gem;
Palaces, silver pillars with marble lace between—
Ruinous for your bankers even to dream of them—;

Processions, coronations,—such costumes as we lack
Tongue to describe—seen cobras dance, and watched them kiss
The juggler's mouth; seen women with nails and teeth stained
    black."

V

And then?—and then?

VI

        "You children! Do you want more of this?

Well, then, and most impressive of all: you cannot go
Anywhere, and not witness—it's thrust before your eyes—
On every rung of the ladder, the high as well as the low,
The tedious spectacle of sin-that-never-dies.

[239]

La femme, esclave vile, orgueilleuse et stupide,
Sans rire s'adorant et s'aimant sans dégoût:
L'homme, tyran goulu, paillard, dur et cupide,
Esclave de l'esclave et ruisseau dans l'égout;

Le bourreau qui jouit, le martyr qui sanglote;
La fête qu'assaisonne et parfume le sang;
Le poison du pouvoir énervant le despote,
Et le peuple amoureux du fouet abrutissant;

Plusieurs religions semblables à la nôtre,
Toutes escaladant le ciel; la Sainteté,
Comme en un lit de plume un délicat se vautre,
Dans les clous et le crin cherchant la volupté;

L'Humanité bavarde, ivre de son génie,
Et, folle maintenant comme elle était jadis,
Criant à Dieu, dans sa furibonde agonie:
"O mon semblable, ô mon maître, je te maudis!"

Et les moins sots, hardis amants de la Démence,
Fuyant le grand troupeau parqué par le Destin,
Et se réfugiant dans l'opium immense!
—Tel est du globe entier l'éternel bulletin."

Woman, vile slave, adoring herself, ridiculous
And unaware of it, too stupid and too vain;
And man, the pompous tyrant, greedy, cupidinous
And hard, slave of a slave, and gutter into the drain.

The headsman happy in his work, the victim's shriek;
Banquets where blood has peppered the pot, perfumed the fruits;
Poison of too much power making the despot weak;
The people all in love with the whip which keeps them brutes;

Divers religions, all quite similar to ours,
Each promising salvation and life; Saints everywhere,
Who might as well be wallowing on feather-beds and flowers
As getting so much pleasure from those hair-shirts they wear.

Humanity, still talking too much, drunken and proud
As ever of its talents, to mighty God on high
In anguish and in furious wrath shouting aloud,
'Master, made in my image! I curse Thee! Mayst Thou die!'

Not all, of course, are quite such nit-wits; there are some
Who, sickened by the norm, and paying serious court
To Madness, seeking refuge, turn to opium.
We've been around the world; and this is our report."

VII

Amer savoir, celui qu'on tire du voyage!
Le monde, monotone et petit, aujourd'hui,
Hier, demain, toujours, nous fait voir notre image:
Une oasis d'horreur dans un désert d'ennui!

Faut-il partir? rester? Si tu peux rester, reste;
Pars, s'il le faut. L'un court, et l'autre se tapit
Pour tromper l'ennemi vigilant et funeste,
Le Temps! Il est, hélas! des coureurs sans répit,

Comme le Juif errant et comme les apôtres,
A qui rien ne suffit, ni wagon ni vaisseau,
Pour fuir ce rétiaire infâme; il en est d'autres
Qui savent le tuer sans quitter leur berceau.

Lorsque enfin il mettra le pied sur notre échine,
Nous pourrons espérer et crier: En avant!
De même qu'autrefois nous partions pour la Chine,
Les yeux fixés au large et les cheveux au vent,

Nous nous embarquerons sur la mer des Ténèbres
Avec le cœur joyeux d'un jeune passager.
Entendez-vous ces voix, charmantes et funèbres,
Qui chantent: "Par ici! vous qui voulez manger

VII

Bitter the knowledge gained from travel. . . . What am I?
The small monotonous world reflects me everywhere:
Yesterday, now, tomorrow, for ever—in a dry
Desert of boredom, an oasis of despair!

Shall I go on?—stay here? Stay here, exhausted man!
Yet, if you must, go on—keep under cover—flee—
Try to outwit the watchful enemy if you can—
Sepulchral Time! Alas, how many there must be

Constrained like the apostles, like the wandering Jew,
To journey without respite over dust and foam
To dodge the net of Time!—and there are others, who
Have quietly killed him, never having stirred from home.

Yet, when his foot is on our spine, one hope at least
Remains: wriggle from under! Onward! The untrod track!
Just as we once set forth for China and points east,
Wide eyes on the wide sea, and hair blown stiffly back,

We shall embark upon the Sea of Shadows, gay
As a young passenger on his first voyage out. . . .
What are those sweet, funereal voices? "Come this way,
All ye that are in trouble!—all ye that are in doubt!

Le Lotus parfumé! c'est ici qu'on vendange
Les fruits miraculeux dont votre cœur a faim;
Venez vous enivrer de la douceur étrange
De cette après-midi qui n'a jamais de fin?"

A l'accent familier nous devinons le spectre;
Nos Pylades là-bas tendent leurs bras vers nous.
"Pour rafraîchir ton cœur nage vers ton Électre!"
Dit celle dont jadis nous baisions les genoux.

VIII

O Mort, vieux capitaine, il est temps! levons l'ancre!
Ce pays nous ennuie, ô Mort! Appareillons!
Si le ciel et la mer sont noirs comme de l'encre,
Nos cœurs que tu connais sont remplis de rayons!

Verse-nous ton poison pour qu'il nous réconforte!
Nous voulons, tant ce feu nous brûle le cerveau,
Plonger au fond du gouffre, Enfer ou Ciel, qu'importe?
Au fond de l'Inconnu pour trouver du nouveau!

"Ye that would drink of Lethe and eat of Lotus-flowers,
Here are miraculous fruits!—here, harvested, are piled
All things the heart has missed! Drink, through the long, sweet hours
Of that clear afternoon never by dusk defiled!"

We know this ghost—those accents!—Pylades! comforter
And friend!—his arms outstretched!—ah, and this ghost we know,
That calls, "I am Electra! Come!"—the voice of her
Whose lost, belovèd knees we kissed so long ago.

VIII

Oh, Death, old captain, hoist the anchor! Come, cast off!
We've seen this country, Death! We're sick of it! Let's go!
The sky is black; black is the curling crest, the trough
Of the deep wave; yet crowd the sail on, even so!

Pour us your poison wine that makes us feel like gods!
Our brains are burning up!—there's nothing left to do
But plunge into the void!—hell? heaven?—what's the odds?
We're bound for the Unknown, in search of something new!

E. ST. V. M.

LES MÉTAMORPHOSES DU VAMPIRE

La femme cependant de sa bouche de fraise,
En se tordant ainsi qu'un serpent sur la braise,
Et pétrissant ses seins sur le fer de son busc,
Laissait couler ces mots tout imprégnés de musc:
—"Moi, j'ai la lèvre humide, et je sais la science
De perdre au fond d'un lit l'antique conscience.
Je sèche tous les pleurs sur mes seins triomphants
Et fais rire les vieux du rire des enfants.
Je remplace, pour qui me voit nue et sans voiles,
La lune, le soleil, le ciel et les étoiles!
Je suis, mon cher savant, si docte aux voluptés,
Lorsque j'étouffe un homme en mes bras veloutés,
Ou lorsque j'abandonne aux morsures mon buste,
Timide et libertine, et fragile et robuste,
Que sur ces matelas qui se pâment d'émoi
Les Anges impuissants se damneraient pour moi!"

Quand elle eut de mes os sucé toute la moelle,
Et que languissamment je me tournai vers elle
Pour lui rendre un baiser d'amour, je ne vis plus
Qu'une outre aux flancs gluants, toute pleine de pus!

METAMORPHOSES OF THE VAMPIRE

Meanwhile from her red mouth the woman, in husky tones,
Twisting her body like a serpent upon hot stones
And straining her white breasts from their imprisonment,
Let fall these words, as potent as a heavy scent:
"My lips are moist and yielding, and I know the way
To keep the antique demon of remorse at bay.
All sorrows die upon my bosom. I can make
Old men laugh happily as children for my sake.
For him who sees me naked in my tresses, I
Replace the sun, the moon, and all the stars of the sky!
Believe me, learnèd sir, I am so deeply skilled
That when I wind a lover in my soft arms, and yield
My breasts like two ripe fruits for his devouring—both
Shy and voluptuous, insatiable and loath—
Upon this bed that groans and sighs luxuriously
Even the impotent angels would be damned for me!"

When she had drained me of my very marrow, and cold
And weak, I turned to give her one more kiss—behold,
There at my side was nothing but a hideous
Putrescent thing, all faceless and exuding pus.

Je fermai les deux yeux dans ma froide épouvante,
Et, quand je les rouvris à la clarté vivante,
A mes côtés, au lieu du mannequin puissant
Qui semblait avoir fait provision de sang,
Tremblaient confusément des débris de squelette,
Qui d'eux-mêmes rendaient le cri d'une girouette
Ou d'une enseigne, au bout d'une tringle de fer,
Que balance le vent pendant les nuits d'hiver.

I closed my eyes and mercifully swooned till day:
And when I looked at morning for that beast of prey
Who seemed to have replenished her arteries from my own,
The wan, disjointed fragments of a skeleton
Wagged up and down in a lewd posture where she had lain,
Rattling with each convulsion like a weathervane
Or an old sign that creaks upon its bracket, right
Mournfully in the wind upon a winter's night.

G. D.

L'ENNEMI

Ma jeunesse ne fut qu'un ténébreux orage,
Traversé çà et là par de brillants soleils;
Le tonnerre et la pluie ont fait un tel ravage
Qu'il reste en mon jardin bien peu de fruits vermeils.

Voilà que j'ai touché l'automne des idées,
Et qu'il faut employer la pelle et les râteaux
Pour rassembler à neuf les terres inondées,
Où l'eau creuse des trous grands comme des tombeaux.

Et qui sait si les fleurs nouvelles que je rêve
Trouveront dans ce sol lavé comme une grève
Le mystique aliment qui ferait leur vigueur?

—O douleur! ô douleur! Le Temps mange la vie,
Et l'obscur Ennemi qui nous ronge le cœur
Du sang que nous perdons croît et se fortifie!

THE ENEMY

I think of my gone youth as of a stormy sky
Infrequently transpierced by a benignant sun;
Tempest and hail have done their work; and what have I?—
How many fruits in my torn garden?—scarcely one.

And now that I approach the autumn of my mind,
And must reclaim once more the inundated earth—
Washed into stony trenches deep as graves—I find
I wield the rake and hoe, asking, "What is it worth?"

Who can assure me, these new flowers for which I toil
Will find in the disturbed and reconstructed soil
That mystic aliment on which alone they thrive?

Oh, anguish, anguish! Time eats up all things alive;
And that unseen, dark Enemy, upon the spilled
Bright blood we could not spare, battens, and is fulfilled.

E. ST. V. M.

LA CLOCHE FÊLÉE

Il est amer et doux, pendant les nuits d'hiver,
D'écouter près du feu qui palpite et qui fume
Les souvenirs lointains lentement s'élever
Au bruit des carillons qui chantent dans la brume.

Bienheureuse la cloche au gosier vigoureux
Qui, malgré sa vieillesse, alerte et bien portante,
Jette fidèlement son cri religieux,
Ainsi qu'un vieux soldat qui veille sous la tente!

Moi, mon âme est fêlée, et lorsqu'en ses ennuis
Elle veut de ses chants peupler l'air froid des nuits,
Il arrive souvent que sa voix affaiblie

Semble le râle épais d'un blessé qu'on oublie
Au bord d'un lac de sang, sous un grand tas de morts,
Et qui meurt, sans bouger, dans d'immenses efforts.

THE CRACKED BELL

Bitter and sweet it is on these long winter nights
To sit before the fire and watch the smoking log
Beat like a heart; and hear our lost, our mute delights
Call with the carillons that ring out in the fog.

What certitude, what health, sounds from that brazen throat,
In spite of age and rust, alert! O happy bell,
Sending into the dark your clear religious note,
Like an old soldier crying through the night, "All's well!"

I am not thus; my soul is cracked across by care;
Its voice, that once could clang upon this icy air,
Has lost the power, it seems,—comes faintly forth, instead,

As from the rattling throat of a hurt man who lies
Beside a lake of blood, under a heap of dead,
And cannot stir, and in prodigious struggling dies.

E. ST. V. M.

LE GOUT DU NÉANT

Morne esprit, autrefois amoureux de la lutte,
L'Espoir, dont l'éperon attisait ton ardeur,
Ne veut plus t'enfourcher! Couche-toi sans pudeur,
Vieux cheval dont le pied à chaque obstacle butte.

Résigne-toi, mon cœur; dors ton sommeil de brute.

Esprit vaincu, fourbu! Pour toi, vieux maraudeur,
L'amour n'a plus de goût, non plus que la dispute;
Adieu donc, chants du cuivre et soupirs de la flûte!
Plaisirs, ne tentez plus un cœur sombre et boudeur!

Le Printemps adorable a perdu son odeur!

Et le Temps m'engloutit minute par minute,
Comme la neige immense un corps pris de roideur;
Je contemple d'en haut le globe en sa rondeur,
Et je n'y cherche plus l'abri d'une cahute!

Avalanche, veux-tu m'emporter dans ta chute?

ANNIHILATION

Poor weary soul! To think how thou wouldst plunge and leap
When the bright spur of Hope into thy flank was pressed!
He has unsaddled thee for good. Lie down and rest,
Old spavined horse, old nag not worthy of thy keep.

Thou, too, my heart, lie down and sleep thy bestial sleep.

And thou, my mind, old highwayman, thou who didst fling
Thyself from ambush upon every joy, go thou
And skulk in peace. No pleasure will come near thee now;
No joy can tempt so sombre and uncouth a thing.

Gone, gone: even that infallible sweet thrill of spring!

Time blots me out, as flakes on freezing bodies fall;
I see the whole round world, with every animal,
And every flower, and every leaf on every branch,
And there is absolutely nothing I like at all.

Come down and carry me away, O avalanche.

G. D.

[255]

LE MORT JOYEUX

Dans une terre grasse et pleine d'escargots
Je veux creuser moi-même une fosse profonde,
Où je puisse à loisir étaler mes vieux os
Et dormir dans l'oubli comme un requin dans l'onde.

Je hais les testaments et je hais les tombeaux;
Plutôt que d'implorer une larme du monde,
Vivant, j'aimerais mieux inviter les corbeaux
A saigner tous les bouts de ma carcasse immonde.

O vers! noirs compagnons sans oreille et sans yeux,
Voyez venir à vous un mort libre et joyeux;
Philosophes viveurs, fils de la pourriture,

A travers ma ruine allez donc sans remords,
Et dites-moi s'il est encor quelque torture
Pour ce vieux corps sans âme et mort parmi les morts?

THE HAPPY DEAD MAN

Slowly, luxuriously, I will hollow a deep grave,
With my own hands, in rich black snail-frequented soil,
And lay me down, forspent with that voluptuous toil,
And go to sleep, as happy as a shark in the wave.

No funeral for me, no sepulchre, no hymns;
Rather than beg for pity when alive, God knows,
I have lain sick and shelterless, and let the crows
Stab to their hearts' content at my lean festering limbs.

O worms! my small black comrades without ears or eyes,
Taste now for once a mortal who lies down in bliss.
O blithe materialists! O vermin of my last bed!

Come, march remorselessly through me. Come, and devise
Some curious new torment, if you can, for this
Old body without soul and deader than the dead.

G. D.

BÉNÉDICTION

Lorsque, par un décret des puissances suprêmes,
Le Poète apparaît en ce monde ennuyé,
Sa mère épouvantée et pleine de blasphèmes
Crispe ses poings vers Dieu, qui la prend en pitié :

"Ah! que n'ai-je mis bas tout un nœud de vipères,
Plutôt que de nourrir cette dérision!
Maudite soit la nuit aux plaisirs éphémères
Où mon ventre a conçu mon expiation!

"Puisque tu m'as choisie entre toutes les femmes
Pour être le dégoût de mon triste mari,
Et que je ne puis pas rejeter dans les flammes,
Comme un billet d'amour, ce monstre rabougri,

"Je ferai rejaillir ta haine qui m'accable
Sur l'instrument maudit de tes méchancetés,
Et je tordrai si bien cet arbre misérable
Qu'il ne pourra pousser ses boutons empestés!"

BENEDICTION

When, on a certain day, into this harassed world
The Poet, by decree of the high powers, was born,
His mother, overwhelmed by shame and fury, hurled
These blasphemies at God, clenching her fists in scorn:

"Would I had whelped a knot of vipers,—at the worst
'Twere better than this runt that whines and snivels there!
Oh, cursèd be that night of pleasure, thrice accurst
My womb, that has conceived and nourished my despair!

"Since, of all mortal women, it would seem my fate
To be my saddened husband's horror and disgust;
And since I may not toss this monster in the grate—
Like any crumpled letter, reeking of stale lust—

"Upon his helpless form, whereby Thou humblest me,
I shall divert Thy hatred in one raging flood;
And I shall twist so well this miserable tree
That it shall not put forth one pestilential bud!"

Elle ravale ainsi l'écume de sa haine,
Et, ne comprenant pas les desseins éternels,
Elle-même prépare au fond de la Géhenne
Les bûchers consacrés aux crimes maternels.

Pourtant, sous la tutelle invisible d'un Ange,
L'Enfant déshérité s'enivre de soleil,
Et dans tout ce qu'il boit et dans tout ce qu'il mange
Retrouve l'ambroisie et le nectar vermeil.

Il joue avec le vent, cause avec le nuage
Et s'enivre en chantant du chemin de la croix;
Et l'Esprit qui le suit dans son pèlerinage
Pleure de le voir gai comme un oiseau des bois.

Tous ceux qu'il veut aimer l'observent avec crainte,
Ou bien, s'enhardissant de sa tranquillité,
Cherchent à qui saura lui tirer une plainte,
Et font sur lui l'essai de leur férocité.

Dans le pain et le vin destinés à sa bouche
Ils mêlent de la cendre avec d'impurs crachats;
Avec hypocrisie ils jettent ce qu'il touche,
Et s'accusent d'avoir mis leurs pieds dans ses pas.

Thus did she foam with anger, railing, swallowing froth;
And, unaware of what the mighty powers had willed,
She set about to draw Gehenna on them both,
Eyeing the fire, considering how he might be killed.

Meantime, above the child an unseen angel beats
His wings, and the poor waif runs laughing in the sun;
And everything he drinks and everything he eats
Are nectar and ambrosia to this hapless one.

Companioned by the wind, conversing with the cloud,
Along the highway to the Cross his song is heard;
And the bright Spirit, following him, weeps aloud
To see him hop so gaily, like a little bird.

Those whom he longs to love observe him with constraint
And fear, as he grows up; or, seeing how calm he is,
Grow bold, and seek to draw from him some sharp complaint,
Wreaking on him all day their dull ferocities.

Cinders are in his bread, are gritty in his teeth;
Spittle is in his wine. Where his footprints are seen
They hesitate to set their shoes, mincing beneath
Hypocrisy; all things he touched, they call unclean.

Sa femme va criant sur les places publiques :
"Puisqu'il me trouve assez belle pour m'adorer,
Je ferai le métier des idoles antiques,
Et comme elles je veux me faire redorer ;

"Et je me soûlerai de nard, d'encens, de myrrhe,
De génuflexions, de viandes et de vins,
Pour savoir si je puis dans un cœur qui m'admire
Usurper en riant les hommages divins!

"Et, quand je m'ennuîrai de ces farces impies,
Je poserai sur lui ma frêle et forte main ;
Et mes ongles, pareils aux ongles des harpies,
Sauront jusqu'à son cœur se frayer un chemin.

"Comme un tout jeune oiseau qui tremble et qui palpite,
J'arracherai ce cœur tout rouge de son sein,
Et, pour rassasier ma bête favorite,
Je le lui jetterai par terre avec dédain!"

Vers le Ciel, où son œil voit un trône splendide,
Le Poète serein lève ses bras pieux,
Et les vastes éclairs de son esprit lucide
Lui dérobent l'aspect des peuples furieux :

His wife in public places cries, "Since after all
He loves me so, that he's the laughing-stock of men,
I'll make a business of it, be an idol, call
For gold, to have myself regilded now and then!

"And some day, when I'm drunk with frankincense, rich food,
Flattery, genuflexions, spikenard, heady wine,
I'll get from him (while laughing in his face, I could!)
That homage he has kept, so far, for things divine.

"And, when my pleasure in these impious farces fails,
My dainty, terrible hands shall tear his breast apart,
And these long nails of mine, so like to harpies' nails,
Shall dig till they have dug a tunnel to his heart.

"Then, like a young bird, caught and fluttering to be freed,
('Twill make a tasty morsel for my favourite hound)
I'll wrench his heart out, warm and bleeding—let it bleed!—
And drop it, with contempt and loathing, to the ground."

Meanwhile toward Heaven, the goal of his mature desire,
The Poet, oblivious, lifts up his arms in prayer;
His lucid essence flames with lightnings—veiled by fire
Is all the furious world, all the lewd conflict there.

"Soyez béni, mon Dieu, qui donnez la souffrance
Comme un divin remède à nos impuretés,
Et comme la meilleure et la plus pure essence
Qui prépare les forts aux saintes voluptés!

"Je sais que vous gardez une place au Poète
Dans les rangs bienheureux des saintes Légions,
Et que vous l'invitez à l'éternelle fête
Des Trônes, des Vertus, des Dominations.

"Je sais que la douleur est la noblesse unique
Où ne mordront jamais la terre et les enfers,
Et qu'il faut pour tresser ma couronne mystique
Imposer tous les temps et tous les univers.

"Mais les bijoux perdus de l'antique Palmyre,
Les métaux inconnus, les perles de la mer,
Par votre main montés, ne pourraient pas suffire
A ce beau diadème éblouissant et clair;

"Car il ne sera fait que de pure lumière,
Puisée au foyer saint des rayons primitifs,
Et dont les yeux mortels, dans leur splendeur entière,
Ne sont que des miroirs obscurcis et plaintifs!"

"Be praised, Almighty God, that givest to faulty me
This suffering, to purge my spirit of its sin,
To fortify my puny strength, to bid me see
Pure Faith, and what voluptuous blisses dwell therein.

"I know that in those ranks on ranks of happy blest
The Poet shall have some place among Thy Seraphim;
And that Thou wilt at length to the eternal feast .
Of Virtues, Thrones and Dominations, summon him.

"I know, Pain is the one nobility we have
Which not the hungry ground nor hell shall ever gnaw;
I know that space and time, beyond the temporal grave,
Weave me a mystic crown, free from all earthly flaw.

"Not emeralds, not all the pearls of the deep sea,
All the rare metals, every lost and buried gem
Antique Palmyra hides, could ever seem to me
So beautiful as that clear glittering diadem.

"Of Light, of Light alone, it will be fashioned, Light
Drawn from the holy fount, rays primitive and pure,
Whereof the eyes of mortal men, so starry bright,
Are but the mirrors, mirrors cloudy and obscure."

E. ST. V. M.

BIOGRAPHICAL NOTE

CHARLES BAUDELAIRE

A TRAGEDY

DRAMATIS PERSONAE

CHARLES BAUDELAIRE, *a poet and critic*
GEN. AUPICK, *his step-father*
M. ANCELLE, *a solicitor, guardian of Charles' fortune*
POULET-MALASSIS, *Charles' friend and publisher*
M. ARONDEL, *a money-lender*
DAUMIER ⎫
DELACROIX ⎬ *painters, friends of Charles*
MANET ⎭
GAUTIER ⎫
SAINTE-BEUVE ⎬ *writers, friends of Charles*
FLAUBERT ⎭
VICTOR HUGO ⎫
ALFRED DE VIGNY ⎬ *poets*
ALFRED DE MUSSET ⎪
HEINRICH HEINE ⎭
RICHARD WAGNER, *a musician*
EDGAR ALLAN POE, *a voice*
CAROLINE BAUDELAIRE *(afterwards Mme. Aupick) Charles' mother*
MME. SABATIER
JEANNE DUVAL, *a mulattress, Charles' mistress*
     painters, writers, money-lenders, creditors, etc.
     Scene: Mostly Paris. Sometimes Brussels, sometimes Honfleur.
     Time: 1821–1867

IF one were to write a play about the life of Charles Baudelaire, the cast of characters would very possibly read much as I have presented it. In order to avoid for myself the anguish of writing, and for the reader the boredom of reading or endeavouring to read a conventional Biographical Sketch—which I should be bound to do very awkwardly, having but the scantiest of talents for narrative writing of any sort—I shall instead consider here, in the order in which they appear on my play-bill, the persons who were a part of and most deeply influenced Baudelaire's life.

Charles Baudelaire:

Born in Paris, April 9, 1821, the son of well-to-do parents, only child of their marriage. François Baudelaire, Charles' father, would probably not appear in the play, since he died, at the age of about seventy, when the boy was not quite six. François Porché, in his *Vie Douleureuse de Charles Baudelaire*, says that it was from his father, who had lived intimately, in the capacity of companion and tutor, with the *duc de Choiseul-Praslin*, that Baudelaire learned that fastidiousness, that punctiliousness, that cold and elaborate courtesy and outmoded elegance which were to distinguish him throughout his life, and which were so often to be considered as affectation and pose. Gautier wrote of Baudelaire, in his preface to the 1868 edition of *Les Fleurs du Mal*, "His courtesy was excessive to the point of appearing mannered."

Gen. Aupick:

Not quite two years after the death of her first husband Caroline Archimbault-Dufays Baudelaire was married to Commandant Aupick, "a brilliant military man, who for six years had been aide de camp of the prince of Hohenlohe," (Porché) and who was destined to go steadily on from one military honour to another; he was later made ambassador to Madrid, and after that ambassador to Constantinople; he was made colonel, he was made general.

François Baudelaire had been thirty-four years older than his bride; M. Aupick was only a few years her senior. The boy Charles, who for nearly two years had been alone with his young mother, was passionately in love with her. "What is it," he wrote in 1860 to Poulet-Malassis, "what is it that the child loves so passionately in his mother . . . ? Is it simply the being who feeds him, combs him, bathes him and rocks him? *It is also the caresses and the sensuous voluptuousness.*—He loves his mother . . . for the agreeable tickling of satin and fur, for the perfume of her breast and hair, for the clicking of jewels . . ." Charles Baudelaire at the age of seven was deceived and betrayed in love; and he hated his mother's husband immediately with a furious jealousy and scorn which never lessened. One day when Charles was nineteen his mother was giving a dinner-party. During the dinner the boy said something which Gen. Aupick considered improper, and was sharply rebuked for it. Porché describes what followed: "About the table, a profound silence; Baudelaire, humiliated, rose, white with rage . . . and said to his step-father, "Sir, you are gravely at fault. This calls for correction; and I am going to do myself the honour of strangling you." Before he could proceed to do so Gen. Aupick struck him, and he was led away and locked up in his room.

Two years previously, the insubordination to discipline of the young Baudelaire at the college Louis-Le-Grand in Paris had brought about his expulsion. Gen. Aupick, but for the intercession of his wife, would have sent the boy to a reform-school. Now, definitely, something must be done. On the ninth of June, 1841, Baudelaire was taken to Bordeaux and put, under special charge of the captain, aboard a ship bound for Calcutta.

Nine months after setting sail on the *Paquebot des Mers du Sud* Baudelaire was back in Paris. He had never reached Calcutta. Off the Cape of Good Hope the vessel had run into a terrific storm. "Never in all my long life as a sailor have I encountered the like of it," said the captain in his report. For five days the ship wallowed helplessly in the sea; a mast was broken and went overboard, taking part of the sail with it, the cabins were flooded. Finally the weather cleared, and the disabled vessel proceeded to *l'île Maurice*, where she put in for repairs. Porché says here that according to the report of the captain, throughout the course of the storm his young passenger never once lost his calmness and courtesy; that Captain Saur, "who had good reason to know what bravery was," was struck with admiration of the boy's courage. Baudelaire refused to continue with the journey. He was finally persuaded to proceed with the ship as far as *l'île Bourbon*, on the understanding that if there he still persisted in his desire to return to France, every facility would be given him. Baudelaire at Bourbon remained for twenty days in the packet-boat anchored off Saint-Denis. He was sick from weariness and nostalgia, sick from the frightful heat of the climate; he never set foot on shore. When the ship proceeded on its way to Calcutta he was not on board; he had been transferred to the *Alcide*, bound for Bordeaux.

M. ANCELLE:

On the ninth of April, 1842, two months after his return from the east, Baudelaire came into his money. Almost immediately he left home, leaving a letter for his mother, saying that he could no longer bear it to live under the same roof with his step-father, and took rooms in a quiet old part of Paris, on the *île St. Louis*. For several years he had been writing poetry, and he was now determined to devote his life to writing. He began to spend his money very fast. He bought everything that pleased his fancy. He bought engravings; he had his books re-bound in handsome bindings. Théodore de Banville wrote of him at this period: "Charles Baudelaire at twenty—rich, happy, loved, already famous—oh, rare example of a face really divine, uniting . . . all strengths, all the most irresistible seductions." He was elegant in his clothing as in his manner; he spent a great deal of time with his tailor, with his hatter; he was a follower of Beau Brummel, a "dandy."

It was during this period that Baudelaire met Jeanne Duval. He established her in an expensive apartment. In a short time he had gone through half his fortune. His mother and step-father were able to obtain a decree by which the remainder of his money was put in trust for him with a solicitor, who was to give him a certain allowance every month. This solicitor was M. Ancelle, an excellent, conservative, kind-hearted old man, who began at once to lecture for the good of his soul the extremely indignant and irritated young poet. In a fury of exasperation Baudelaire wrote to his mother, "This is too much. I'm going to slap his face. I'm going to slap his face in front of his wife and daughters. I'm going to slap his face at four o'clock; it's now two-thirty."

From this moment Baudelaire was always in debt, and moving from hotel to hotel in Paris, leaving no address, in order to dodge his creditors. His letters to Ancelle are filled with weary and exasperated requests for advances on his monthly allowance, which even when he was very ill were seldom forthcoming. In 1853 he wrote to Ancelle from Brussels, "You congratulate me upon my health. For eight days I have suffered the tortures of the damned. For two months, generally at midnight, every night I am taken with fever. The long hours pass in a continual shivering and cold; finally in the morning I fall asleep from fatigue, not having been able to profit by my insomnia by working; and I wake up late, drenched with perspiration, worn out from having slept. For the last week the pain has been worse.— Finally, there are a great many small expenses, aside from the hotel, which I am unable to meet except through some ridiculous ruse: tobacco, writing-paper, postage-stamps, having my clothes mended, etc. For example, the dream of possessing some wine of quinine has become an obsession with me.—I can procure nothing of all that. (Between parentheses, I beg you to say nothing of all this to my mother. You know what a terrible imagination she has, *So, not a word.*——)

"I was speaking to you of the humiliation of my small necessities. Forgive me for calling your attention in passing that your letters . . . are always insufficiently stamped. That I should mention this to you is certainly a sign of my degradation. When the *concierge* says to me, 'Sir, there are forty centimes to pay on this,' I am very much embarrassed. You stamp as if you were sending your letter into a department of France. It is a red stamp that you must put on, or two blue ones. Pardon!"

In the course of years of hopeless and painful correspondence with him, Baudelaire came to regard M. Ancelle with a sort of scornful tolerance which finally seemed to grow into a real affection, manifesting itself at times in scoldings and mild abuse.

POULET-MALASSIS:

This was the man who published *Les Fleurs du Mal,* and as close a friend perhaps as their author had. (Baudelaire always referred to the *Flowers* as "they.") Baudelaire seems to have had few close friends. His letters to Poulet-Malassis preceding the publication of his poems show the same fastidiousness and attention to detail which distinguished him in every department of his life. "Today again, I have been unable to write you all I have to say to you. I address you only, in haste, these few observations:

1st. Your inverted commas are turned in a very strange way.

2nd. I recommend to you my dedication, with an infinite love. Something rather slight, delicate, in good proportion.

3rd. Is not your running title too close to the first line of verse? There should be at least as much space between the first verse and the running title as between the stanzas."

"As for my punctuation, remember that it serves to show, not only the sense, but the declamation."

"I know, I repeat, how hateful people make themselves by such nagging as this, but . . . you told me once that you thought, as I do, that in any kind of production nothing is admissible except perfection."

"Your type-setter must be either very headstrong or very stupid. My Roman numerals are always exact."

"You treat me as if I were crazy, but I should just like to see you risk a work of your own in conditions which were not absolutely satisfactory. Your very devoted, and excuse my sadness . . ."

Les Fleurs du Mal were published in the summer of 1857, and were immediately seized by the police. As a result of the trial which followed, both author and publisher were fined, and six of the poems, *Les Bijoux, Le Léthé, A celle qui est trop gai, Lesbos, Femmes Damneés,* and *Les métamorphoses du Vampire,* were suppressed—the edition of 1861 appeared without them.[1]

In 1864 Baudelaire wrote to M. Ancelle from Brussels, where he had gone to give some lectures on contemporary painters and writers, "Many people crowded, with a booby-like curiosity, about the author of *Les Fleurs du Mal.* The author of the *Flowers* in question could not be otherwise than an unnatural eccentric. All this rabble took me for a monster, and, when they saw that I was cold, moderate and polite—and that I had a horror of freethinkers, progress, and the whole modern idiocy—they decreed (so I imagine) that I *was not the author of my book.* What comic confusion between author and subject! This cursed book (*of which I am very proud*) is, it would seem, very obscure, very unintelligible! I shall bear for a long time the burden of having dared to paint evil with some talent."

In February, 1866, he wrote to M. Ancelle (one of the last letters he wrote with his own hand), "Is it necessary to tell you, you who have not guessed it any more than the others, that into this *atrocious* book I put *all my heart, all my tenderness, all my religion* (travestied), *all my hatred?* It is true that I shall write the contrary, that I shall swear by all the *gods* that it is a book *of pure art, of monkey-shines, of hocus-pocus,* and I shall lie like an extractor of teeth."

M. ARONDEL:

When Baudelaire first met and fell in love with Jeanne Duval, and took rooms for her near his own, he had not sufficient ready money to buy for her the furniture, the jewels, etc. which he wished to give her. He borrowed money from a man named Arondel. From that moment the shadow of Arondel and other usurers was over his life.

[1] Five of these poems are printed in this collection.

Daumier, Delacroix, Manet :

Baudelaire was a brilliant critic not only of literature, but also of painting. In my cast of characters I have called these painters "friends of Charles." More properly speaking, it was he who was their friend. He admired all three, and was largely responsible, through his critical articles, for establishing them before the public as men of talent. Delacroix was already beginning to be recognized, but Manet and Daumier were meeting with much discouragement and having a hard time to get along. Baudelaire was never too busy or too ill to rush to the aid of artists whom he admired. His enthusiasm for fine art and pleasure in it was the strongest thing in his nature. To try to get a job for Daumier, "kicked out of *Charivari* in the middle of the month, and with only the half-month's pay," to defend Manet from the charge of being an imitator of Goya and El Greco—such things as these were the really important things in his life.

Gautier, Sainte-Beuve, Flaubert :

It was to Théophile Gautier that Baudelaire dedicated the first edition of *Les Fleurs du Mal*. "To the Impeccable Poet, to the Perfect Magician-of-Letters," the dedication begins. The definitive edition of *Les Fleurs du Mal* has a long preface by Gautier, full of sorrow at Baudelaire's death and admiration of his talent, but apparently somewhat bewildered by the subtlety of that talent, deploring the fact that Baudelaire had departed in his sonnets from the classical form of Pierre de Ronsard, and expending some energy in an effort to show that Baudelaire's death was in no way influenced by the excessive use of drugs, suggesting in fact that Baudelaire had never taken opium at all. Whether or not Baudelaire was in the habit of taking opium solely for the purpose of deadening pain, he was most certainly in the habit of taking opium. He wrote to M. Ancelle in December 1865, "A doctor whom I had in, was ignorant that I had for a long time been accustomed to the use of opium . . . and that is why I was obliged to double and to quadruple the prescribed doses."

For Sainte-Beuve, *l'oncle Beuve*, as he called him, Baudelaire seems to have had a very real and deep affection; the fact that Uncle Beuve was always extremely adroit at slipping out of any responsibility toward his spiritual nephew, and so cautious for his own reputation that nothing was able to corner him into the smallest public statement which might have advanced the reputation of Baudelaire, seems never to have struck with any force the younger poet who had admired the poetry of Sainte-Beuve when he was a boy at school. It is possible that the famous author of the *Causeries du Lundi* saw little excellent in *Les Fleurs du Mal* and was embarrassed by their author's devotion to him; but if his position on the subject remains rather fuddled and shapeless, it is because he himself neglected with considerable patience and cunning to say what he thought.

In June, 1860, Baudelaire wrote to Flaubert, "One of these days, if you permit me, when on my way to Honfleur, I will stop off at Rouen, but, as I presume that you are like me, and that you hate being surprised, I will let you know well in advance.

"You tell me that I do a great deal of work. Are you making fun of me? Many people, not counting myself, think that I don't do so very much.

"To work, is to work ceaselessly, it is to have no more feeling, no more revery, and it is to be a pure will, always in motion. Perhaps I shall get there.

"I have always dreamed of reading (in its entirety) *The Temptation* and another singular book, of which you have not published even a line, (*November*.) And how is *Carthage* getting along?"

In a letter to Poulet-Malassis (December, 1862) he said, "As for *Salammbo* [doubtless the *Carthage* of the letter to Flaubert], a great, great success. An edition of two thousand exhausted in two days.—*There are those who reproach Flaubert his imitation of ancient authors*. What Flaubert has done, he alone could do. Much too much bric-a-brac, but many grandeurs, epical, historical, political, even animal. Something astonishing in this gesticulation of all living beings."

Victor Hugo, Alfred de Vigny, Alfred de Musset, Heinrich Heine:

When Charles Baudelaire was born, Victor Hugo, a serious young man of twenty, was already writing religious and political poems, poems about the unfortunate little Louis XVII, about children accidentally shot in the street; Alfred de Musset, a beautiful blond boy of eleven, was going to school and reading Byron; Verlaine was not yet born; Keats, at the age of twenty-six, had just died in Rome; Shelley, shocked by the death of Keats, was writing *Adonais* in his memory, unaware that he himself, at the age of twenty-nine, had only one more year to live; Thomas de Quincey, innocent and hungry, was wandering the streets of London with a kind-hearted little prostitute named Ann; in America a destitute orphan of thirteen named Edgar Poe had been adopted by a kind-hearted gentleman named Allan.

As a boy, Baudelaire read the poetry of Victor Hugo and admired it. As he grew older and his own talent began to take so different a turn he must to some extent have lost his interest in such poetry as that of Hugo, although he never ceased to respect it. "One can at the same time possess a special sort of genius and be an ass. Victor Hugo has thoroughly proved that," he wrote in a letter. And again, "Hugo is coming to live in Brussels"; (Hugo had been living in exile on the island of Guernesey); "he and the ocean seem to have had a falling-out. Whether he wasn't able to stand the ocean, or the ocean got bored with him, I can't say."

Alfred de Musset is the one poet, with the exception of Beranger, whom he sometimes mentions, of whom Baudelaire always spoke slightingly. "I felt somewhat surprised," he wrote to Armand Fraisse in 1857, "to see your admiration for de Musset. Except at the age of first communion, that is to say, the age when everything that has to do with prostitutes and with silk ladders is a form of religion, I have never been able to suffer this master of fops, his impudence of a spoiled child invoking heaven and hell for his table d'hôte adventures; his out-pouring, muddy with faults in grammar and in prosody; finally his total inability to comprehend the toil required to make a revery into a work of art." He wrote to Ancelle from Brussels, "How can you be such a child as not to realize that France does not care for poetry, for real poetry, but only for the work of sloppy fellows like Beranger and de Musset."

In 1841, when Baudelaire was twenty, Victor Hugo was taken into the *Académie française*. Eleven years later Alfred de Musset became a member of the Academy. In 1861 Baudelaire tried to get into the Academy and failed, was practically laughed out of it; the members of the Academy did not take him seriously, were not at home when he called, etc. Alfred de Vigny, old and ill as he was at the time, seems to have been the only one to receive Baudelaire with courtesy and interest. He made himself not at home to all other visitors, and talked with the younger poet for hours, in appreciation of his talent and understanding of its subtlety.

Though Baudelaire himself says of this attempt, in a letter to Arsène Houssaye, that he has no hope, and is doing it only because he takes pleasure in being the goat ("à me faire bouc") for all unfortunate men of letters, there is no doubt that he cared greatly about becoming a member of the *Académie française*, and was wounded and humiliated by the reception accorded his application. The fact that Victor Hugo and Alfred de Musset had both been admitted to the distinguished gathering, must have been a bitter crust for the author of *Les Fleurs du Mal* to gnaw. I do not think, however, that Baudelaire's remark in a letter to Ancelle, that unpleasant reports were being circulated about him in Brussels, doubtless by someone in "Hugo's gang," and his unfailingly contemptuous remarks about that "languorous undertaker" de Musset, have much if anything to do with any personal jealousy. That is to say, Baudelaire was undoubtedly jealous of de Musset's success, but only because he thought it undeserved; if he had liked de Musset's poetry, he would have been incapable of being jealous of him. Baudelaire appears to me to have had no professional jealousy whatsoever; the moment he read a book or looked at a painting which he thought excellent, all other considerations were automatically swallowed up in undiluted pleasure and excitement. In his enthusiasm for Gautier, for Flaubert, for Heinrich Heine, for Poe, for Wagner, for Daumier, for everybody whom he admired, he forgot himself and lost himself entirely.

RICHARD WAGNER:

Charles Baudelaire was one of those present at the famous *Pasdeloup* concerts in Paris in January and February, 1860, when for the first time the music of Wagner was played there; he was present at the *Opéra* in March, 1861, when *Tannhauser* was presented. And he was one of those comparatively few members of the audience who insisted from the first that this man who had written the music was a great man. In a letter to Champfleury written February 28, 1860, he said, "If you see Wagner before I do, tell him that it will be for me a great happiness to grasp the hand of a man of genius, insulted by all the populace of trivial minds." In a letter to Poulet-Malassis, written on the sixteenth of the same month, he had said, "I don't dare talk about Wagner any more; everybody has made such fun of me. It was one of the great raptures of my life, that music; not for fifteen years had I felt myself so carried away." (What was it that had happened fifteen years before which meant so much to him? I think he is thinking of his discovery of the writings of Poe.)

EDGAR ALLAN POE:

Now we come to the man whose writing had so great an effect upon the thought and upon the life of Baudelaire that many people, a great many French people among them, consider Baudelaire to have been the spiritual child of Poe, a vehicle and a further expression simply of the American poet who had been dead for some time when Baudelaire became acquainted with his works. This is going far. When the French poet first made the acquaintance of the writings of Poe he was twenty-five years old, and had already written some of his most characteristic verse. But see what Baudelaire himself had to say about it, in a typical letter written in defense of one of his painter friends who, as I mentioned earlier, had been accused of imitating Goya and El Greco: "M. Manet has never seen a *Goya*; M. Manet has never seen a *Greco*. Do you doubt that such astonishing geometrical parallelisms can present themselves in nature? Very well! They accuse me, me, of imitating Edgar Poe! Do you know why I so patiently translated Poe?—*Because he resembled me.* The first time that I opened a book of his I saw, with awe and rapture, not only subjects dreamed by me, but *sentences*, thought by me, and written by him, twenty years before."

Baudelaire made it the patient and worshipful task of half his writing years to translate the prose of Poe into French, to present to the European public a writer whom he considered to be a genius unappreciated at home. That Baudelaire should have been fascinated by the mind of Poe is natural, and if he had undergone no influence from the work of a poet he so much admired would have been remarkable; nevertheless one has only to compare the poetry of the two poets to be at once aware that Baudelaire was not rewriting Poe.

CAROLINE BAUDELAIRE (AFTERWARDS MME. AUPICK):

I have spoken earlier of Baudelaire's mother, and of his love for her. He never stopped loving her, and throughout his life he saw as much of her as he was able to do; she was absent from Paris much of the time, of course, in Madrid, in Constantinople, a charming and apparently very popular ambassadress. Baudelaire always remained convinced that she had abandoned him. His dedication of his translation of Poe to Poe's mother-in-law, Maria Clemm, who had been so much interested in the work of her daughter's husband and had been so kind and loving to him, who had been to Poe just what Baudelaire thought a mother should be, although she was only Poe's mother-in-law, is full of self-pity and bitterness; it is one of the least attractive pieces of prose that Baudelaire wrote; it was a subject upon which he could not write without bias. Baudelaire seems not to have been aware that whether or not his mother had ever married for the second time, she was bound to fail him sooner or later in a very important way: she was incapable of interesting herself in his writing; she had no idea as to whether he wrote well or ill, and she had no apparatus for judging. She always remained to him the proverbial hen who has hatched a duckling: to see him swimming about all alone like that made her nervous; and besides, she had planned such a handsome career for him on shore. She helped him sometimes with money, as much as she felt she could; later in her life she was forced to make her own economies; but the economizing of the rich never seems quite serious to the poor. Sometimes she came to see him in his shabby quarters, and after one visit she wrote him, saying how pained she had been to see him going to pieces as he was, taking no care of his person, etc. He replied to her in a furious letter: "As for your fears concerning the degradation of my person in poverty, know that, all my life, going in rags or living decently, I have always devoted two hours a day to my toilet. In future do not soil your letters with these stupidities."

Madame Sabatier:

Madame Sabatier was one of several women for whom Baudelaire formed during his life a profound and passionate idealistic attachment. "You are my Guardian Angel, my Madonna, my Muse," this is the way he felt about Madame Sabatier. He wrote several of his most beautiful poems to her; he says to her in a letter, "all the poems between pages 84 and 105 belong to you." "Cheap people are lovers," he wrote to her again; "poets are idolaters. . . . To forget you is not possible. . . . I believe indeed (but I am too much interested) *that fidelity is one of the signs of genius*."

Madame Sabatier put the fidelity of her idolater to a very severe test, when to reward him for his worship, she came down from her niche and suggested that she become his mistress. He was shocked and disappointed; his feeling for her had been of an entirely different nature.

Jeanne Duval:

When Baudelaire was twenty-two, one night after dinner, he dropped in by chance at a little theatre called the *Théâtre du Panthéon*. A play was in progress. A young mulattress came onto the stage and said, "*Madame est servie*." That was her only line in the play. The moment he saw her and heard her voice, Baudelaire began to tremble so from excitement that he could hardly find her name on the program. Her name was Jeanne Duval. The poet sent her flowers, and asked for a rendezvous, which she granted him. Twenty years later, he was still involved with her. She was the great, overwhelming physical passion of his life. He never married. When in his

[277]

letters he speaks of "*ma femme*," it is of this woman that he is speaking.

Jeanne Duval was a mulattress from St. Domingo. She was a woman of no education and no culture, who earned her living for the most part as a common prostitute. Whether or not she was beautiful, it is hard to tell; people who knew her, wrote very differing accounts of her. Apparently she was tall and thin, with magnificent eyes and beautiful heavy hair. Baudelaire made some very interesting sketches of her, some in which she seems to have no charm at all, others in which her seductive quality is plainly felt. His poetry, naturally, is full of her.

Up to the end of his life, even when he was very ill and practically penniless, he never forgot her and never neglected her. In December, 1859, sixteen years after he first met her, he wrote her from his mother's house in Honfleur, "My dear girl, you must not be angry with me that I left Paris so abruptly that I did not get in to see you, to cheer you up a little. You know how worn out with anxiety I have been.—I swear to you that I am coming back in a few days. In the meantime, as I may be absent for a week, and as I don't want you in your condition to be without money even for a day [she had been ill], write to M. Ancelle. I know that I am a little overdrawn on next year, but you know that in spite of his hesitations he is really rather generous.—Now, as I said, I am coming back, and if, as I think, I am *endowed* with a little money, I will try to give you some fun. With these slippery roads don't go out unaccompanied. . . . Don't lose my verses and my articles."

.   .   .   .

In March 1866 Baudelaire, who had been ill for years and during much of the time in pain, was stricken with a partial paralysis, which brought with it a swiftly-growing aphasia. In a short time he was unable to speak at all, although still able, with the aid of a stick, to get about. After a few months he was unable even to leave his bed, and in this condition he existed, unable to speak or write, but with his brain still alive, until the 31st of August, 1867. He died in Paris on that day.

E. ST. V. M.

INDEX OF ORIGINAL FIRST LINES

[279]

Fourmillante cité, cité pleine de rêves—182

Harpagon, qui veillait son père agonisant—134
Horloge! dieu sinistre, effrayant, impassible—36

Il est amer et doux pendant les nuits d'hiver—252
Il est de forts parfums pour qui toute matière—6
Il me semble parfois que mon sang coule à flots—60

J'ai longtemps habité sous de vastes portiques—12
J'ai plus de souvenirs que si j'avais mille ans—150
Je n'ai pas oublié, voisine de la ville—214
Je suis comme le roi d'un pays pluvieux—154
Je te frapperai sans colère—28
Je veux, pour composer chastement mes églogues—174
J'implore ta pitié, Toi, l'unique que j'aime—40

La diane chantait dans les cours des casernes—168
La femme, cependant, de sa bouche de fraise—246
La Maladie et la Mort font des cendres—46
La Nature est un temple où de vivants piliers—196
La pendule, sonnant minuit—130
La servante au grand cœur dont vous étiez jalouse—92
La très-chère etait nue, et, connaissant mon cœur—84
La tribu prophétique aux prunelles ardentes—68
Le Démon, dans ma chambre haute—88
Le long du vieux faubourg, où pendent aux masures—178
Les amoureux fervents et les savants austères—140
Lorsque, par un décret des puissances suprêmes—258
Lorsque tu dormiras, ma belle ténébreuse—26

[281]

Ta tête, ton geste, ton air—142
Tes beaux yeux sont las, pauvre amante—18
Toi qui, comme un coup de couteau—62
Tout homme digne de ce nom—14
Tu mettrais l'univers entier dans ta ruelle—66

Un Ange furieux fond du ciel comme un aigle—108

Viens sur mon cœur, âme cruelle et sourde—2
Vous êtes un beau ciel d'automne, clair et rose—16